DEA

Samples of Kindle Readers Comments

This is a beautiful, honest, funny, gut-wrenching book. Even if Richard couldn't tell his story in such wonderful, lyrical prose, it would still be a memorable story, a reminder to all of us of the fragility of life. It's a testament to the power of love and the memory of love even in the face of the greatest tragedies. *Whistler's Mom*

This book is beautifully written. A friend told me about it and said, 'I bet you can't read this book and not cry." I say the same to anyone else.

This book made me laugh and cry. Not many books do that for me.

Needed a box of tissues close at hand throughout this book – such joy and sadness.

Just finished this amazing book, struggling to see the screen through my tears.

A Man's Summary of the Book

Sitting in his study, alone with his thoughts, a man starts to write a letter to his little granddaughter. Why? Because he wants her to understand, when she gets older, who her mother was, and how much she sacrificed.

It is a harrowing story, but it is also a great "love story" and, in places, humorous. A story of hopes and fears, courage in the face of adversity, disappointments and setbacks, and ultimately, the calm and dignified acceptance that what will be, will be.

But as Richard Rees's story of his daughter unfolds, the reader realises with something nearing dread, that there is an earlier history, a previous parallel which must be understood to be overcome.

The resulting letter, *Dear Abigail*, is both heart-rending and tender by turn, and also an act of healing; an attempt to find meaning in an apparently godless universe, that leads, ultimately, to faith through a miracle of daffodils.

But above all. it is an account of what it means to be human.

Mark Brittain, *Daily Post*

A Woman's Thoughts on the Story

Written as an extended letter to his young granddaughter, Dear Abigail is a moving account of the narrator's loving family life and his struggle to come to terms with unbearable grief. The book is in essence a factional memoir, written as catharsis by Richard Rees in dealing with his own darkest experiences. It is also a touching tribute to his daughter and wife, encapsulating cherished memories of them, for his little granddaughter to read and treasure when she is old enough to understand.

The powerful bond between parent and child is explored: the complete and absolute love that exists within a father for his daughter and his supreme desire to protect her at any cost. Rees gives a first-hand account of his feelings of dread and helplessness when he discovers his daughter is suffering from ovarian cancer. She is just twenty-seven, pretty, bright, bubbly, recently married, pregnant, and a delight. He recounts his two-years of tenderly nursing her and her baby, watching as his daughter bravely loses her battle with the illness, and is left with raw emotion – feeling hopeless, faithless and despairing, and his struggle to come to terms with such a catastrophic loss is heart-rending.

The story will have resonance with those who have experienced intolerable grief following the death of a loved one. Richard comes to realise there is no solution for bereavement; it has happened and will last a lifetime. He does, though, somehow learn to survive, coming to understand the importance of memories as part of the healing process. His memories of his own life and experiences are interwoven throughout the book. They tell the vibrant story of a man who married his childhood sweetheart, had two children and became a successful writer. He also relates the tragic death of his wife from ovarian cancer at the age of just forty-five, making the cruel twist of fate that is later dealt his daughter even more poignant. And with a mixture of humour and affection, he depicts his upbringing in the Welsh countryside, his colourful forbears, his extended family, and his quest to rekindle love.

Dear Abigail is an eloquent and painfully honest book which is both heartbreaking and heart-warming. Immensely sad in parts, there is no over-sentimentality or self-indulgence. By sharing his own experience, Rees touchingly portrays the frailty of the human condition, the immeasurable power of love, and the amazing resilience of the human spirit.

Jaquie Knowles

Dear Abigail,

A letter to a little granddaughter

Also by Richard Rees

The Illuminati Conspiracy

The Reikel Conspiracy

Twice Upon A Thanksgiving

Somebody Wants to Kill Me

Dear Abigail,

A letter to a little granddaughter

RICHARD REES

ISBN: 978-1-5084767-4-0

Front jacket cover design: Louise Payne, www.louisepaynearts.com
Book design: Dean Fetzer, www.gunboss.com

V2

Taken from sonnets by William Shakespeare

But thy eternal summer shall not fade,
Nor lose possession of that fair thou ow'st;
So long as I can breathe, and my eyes can see,
so long lives this, and this gives life to thee.

When to sessions of sweet silent thought,
I summon up remembrance of things past,
Yet, while I think on thee, dear one,
all losses are restored, and sorrows gone.

Dear Abigail is for carers everywhere, for you to know
you are not alone and, that after the grey skies of winter
comes spring. New hope and daffodils.

*All the author's royalties from this book will go to
Target Ovarian Cancer.*

- prologue -

I thought I saw her the other day. My beautiful daughter. It was in the middle of town. Same height, same chic clothes, same stiletto heels clickety-clicking as she walked along the street with her usual confidence, oblivious of heads turning to look at her. Same hair, tawny, with just a touch of gold, Raphaelite tresses cascading halfway down her back.

My heart pounded. I wanted to run to her, aching to hold her once more in my arms, to see her deep, oh-so-expressive eyes looking at me all solemn, as was her way from when she was a child, to kiss her forehead, to soothe away her fears and tell her that it would all be alright this time. Because this time I would take care of it, promise, cross my heart, and make sure it would go away.

Go away for ever. And never return.

And then I remembered that at twenty-one she'd had her glorious hair shorn and changed it to a shorter, cheekier, bouncier style more suited to her personality.

And then she turned her face. And it wasn't Carys at all.

Strangely, instead of pain all I felt was an ache, albeit it a deep ache, which kept gnawing at my heart the whole of my drive home. But the pain that had been my constant companion for over three years now – the pain that cuts at your very soul, that makes you look up into the sky, searching for the God you were taught, as a child, to believe in, the

Abba "Daddy" God who's supposed to be so loving, He knows when even a sparrow falls to the ground, but turned a deaf ear to all my many supplicatory prayers asking Him: 'Why, God, why?' – that pain had finally gone.

And I knew I could allow myself to talk about her at last.

Up to then to talk of her was to want her back, want her back so much it hurt, every good moment of the past over-shadowed by all that happened, knowing that the present was a present built on false hopes, false assumptions, with my body still resident here on earth, but my spirit elsewhere, in limbo.

And I thought again, as I'd so often thought since it first began, of how all of us who loved Carys – Ian and Abigail, Ewen and Jessy, Anne and Tony, even Meryn – for a while there she'd loved her too, in her own way – and me, who'd first held her in my arms when she was less than a minute old – of how we'd all been affected by what happened, tossed hither and thither as if in some black hole in space, before being spewed out on the other side, different creatures, our relationships to each other forever changed.

Changed for the rest of our lives.

That same evening, with the setting sun creating a shaft of red across the wide bay, all the way from the island to the mainland, and back-dropped by the distant mountain peaks towering dark against the deep-blue evening sky, I went outside and sat alone on the patio where on such evenings Carys and I had sat together…and talked…and laughed.

And where she'd shared her dreams with me.

Simple dreams, nothing ambitious, dreams of meeting "someone nice...*and* good looking with it..." and falling in love, of creating a happy home, of having two children, a girl named "Abigail" – always "Abigail" – and a boy named...

But strangely she never could decide on a name for a boy.

It's as if she knew.

As I sat there in the fading light, recollecting Carys's far too short life, I knew that if I was ever to make any sense of it, I must relive those last years. Not just for myself, but for all those many others who loved her and approach me still, asking me to tell "what happened?".

Especially Abigail who even though she's too young to understand, keeps asking me to tell her all about "my Mummy-in-Heaven".

Carys.

My one in a million daughter.

And so I went inside to write Abigail a letter.

For her to have one day when she's old enough to understand.

Telling her all about her "Mummy-in-Heaven".

"**Dear Abigail**", I began.

And as I wrote, I knew it would be more than just a letter.

- one -

Dear Abigail,

Hello, little sixpence. Yes, I know that "little sixpence" is what Mummy-in-Heaven used to call you when you were a tiny, tiny baby, lying asleep in your incubator weighing only four pounds two ounces. I also know (*as if I didn't!*) that you're not a *little* sixpence any more, not now you're five, you're a **BIG** sixpence, and in the blink of an eye, so quickly does time seem to fly, you'll be a shilling, which is **TWICE** as much. But right from the day you were born and it was then for me to care for you, I called you that as well, because that's what you were to us both, Mummy Carys and Gampy, our precious "little sixpence".

But ever since you and Daddy and your new Mummy moved away to live, Gampy misses you so very much, little sweetheart – sorry, **BIG** sweetheart – that writing this letter somehow makes you feel nearer, and anything that can make you seem nearer is exactly what I need right now.

But first, before explaining why I'm writing to you, someone's told me you've got a new baby brother. I'm sure you're excited aren't you? I know how much you've been wanting one to hold. Yes, I know it was a sister you really wanted, but little boys can be cute, too, and just as cuddly to *cwch* – another Welsh word for you, Abigail, pronounced

4

"cooch"; the nearest English has to it is *"cuddle",* but with *oodles and oodles of love and tenderness added.*

What's more, the start of his name: Abe-lin – in keeping with the Romanian part of his blood inherited from Mummy Ileana – sounds like yours:.Abi-gail. No, sixpence, I know it's not spelt the same, it's called phonetics – this time, a new English word for you to learn, but not now, wait until you're a little older and ask Daddy to tell you what it means, seeing I'm no longer there to lift you on my knee and try, as I once used to, to answer all your many, many questions.

But speaking of questions, does Abelin have another name?

I'm sure he does, after your new Gampy maybe – *Bunicu,* as I remember you telling me with that oh-so-earnest expression of yours, that that's what you were going to be calling him (I hope I've spelt it right) – the same as you being also named Rachel, Abigail Rachel, after your real Gammy.

She and I were only eleven when we first met, Abigail, but something passed between us even then; we started going out together at seventeen and married at twenty-one. And just like Mummy Carys was special, Gammy Rachel was also special. Very special. But I'm digressing sweetheart, a fault of mine I know I'll keep repeating throughout this letter, and so I'd best say say "sorry" for them all now in advance, and tell you more about her later.

Meantime, I've sent you a big "Congratulations on Becoming a Sister" card. And a blue one – blue for a boy – to Abelin which says "Welcome into this World". And now that you're a **BIG** girl, and soon be going to proper school, I

5

know you'll be such a help to Mummy Ileana when you get home in the afternoon, bathing and feeding Abelin and *cwching* him when he cries, just like Gampy used to with you, not that you cried much, but then we were big friends weren't we, sixpence, the biggest, do you remember?

But anyway, have lots of fun together the two of you, you'll both be very gifted, able to speak three languages, Welsh, English, and Romanian, to each other. And throughout your lives, always be close, just like Mummy Carys and Uncle Ewen were when they were children and Gampy and Gammy Rachel were young, a happy family looking into a future which seemed to promise so much hope and joy.

Which is partly why I'm writing to you, Abigail.

Because now you're part of a new family with a new Mummy and a new Gampy and Gammy

(*Bunicu* and *Bunica*, I'm sure I've got both right) but with Grandma Anne and Granddad Tony still being the same, then as you grow up you'll naturally be told all the Gannon and Banus family histories, and the funny stories families like to recount when they get together talking in the evenings, especially on special occasions like Christmases and birthdays. But though we – Gampy and Uncle Ewen and Aunty Jessie (and Sara and Nathan, too, who so much miss playing with you) – rarely see you any more, our blood also runs in your veins, and Gampy wants you to know something about us as well, who we are, where we come from, what we're like, for you to know and understand where all those so definite characteristics you inherited from Mummy Carys and Gammy

6

Rachel come from, part of theirs and your Welsh makeup as it were – rather than the Romanian one you're now being mostly brought up to be.

And I, especially, want you to know about your Mummy Carys, Abigail, in a story that began before she and Daddy first met, so that it (as well as what happened after) will be a part of your history. And in telling it, I also want you to always know we're the kind of family who even though we're now apart from you – not just by distance, but by circumstances, too – we will *always* be here for you, should you ever need us for any reason…

Any reason at all, no matter what.

As for this letter, even though I know you won't get to read it until you're, say, sixteen, maybe even eighteen, when I, or Uncle Ewen, decide you are ready to read it, the thought of writing it came to me earlier this evening as I sat on the patio with my memories, watching the red setting sun go down on the horizon, and dark shadows slowly creep across the mountains – mountains that have been here almost since Earth was first formed, and will still be here tens, maybe hundreds of millions of years yet to come.

Compared to their granite immutability our life span is no more than the blink of an eye in time, so quickly does our moment on Earth pass. And as I sat there, gazing at them, it made me aware of my own mortality, and started me thinking: what if I'm not here when you're old enough to decide for yourself, and come looking for us one day as I know you will, wanting to know all about Mummy Carys – and for me to tell you of how *very, very much* she loved you.

She truly did, Abigail. She loved you with all her heart, her soul, her whole being. To quote her, she thought you were: *"The prettiest, bestest, preciousest baby in the whole wide world".*

And it's her blood, Mummy Carys's blood, Abigail, that runs through your veins.

Which means, to repeat, my telling you more than just from when she met Daddy, but will take me further back in time to say something (without, hopefully, digressing *too* much) about where those so endearing traits of hers which are so very strong in you, come from.

A sort of your genetic life story, if you like.

That makes you what you are.

Unique.

Uncle Ewen doesn't know all that happened.

Well, not enough to dot every "i" and cross every "t".

Which is why it's up to me to tell it to you.

As it was to me at the time.

Every heartbeat.

- two -

The day Rachel died I didn't cry.

Not at first.

At first I was too numb to cry.

Forty five, so young, I thought, sitting on the bed beside her, holding her still warm hand, and for the very last time gently kissed her now peaceful face. Free at last from all her pain. Yet far too young.

Ewen and Carys were with us at her ending. She loved them both dearly. Later that day, inside her Bible, we found her last letter to us.

"To My Dearest Family…" it began.

As we read it together the tears finally flowed. All three of us, sitting together on the sofa, our arms around each other, Carys in the middle. Later that evening, under Rachel's now empty pillow, I found a second letter. Addressed just to me, it was a shortlist of second wives. Drawn up, she'd written, because, "Luke…(my middle name, I prefer it, I'm not over keen on any of the abbreviations for "Richard")…we were so happy, and I want the rest of your life to be just as happy. Besides," she'd added (I could just see her, tongue-in-cheek as she wrote it, despite knowing it was her final ps to me) "you'll never manage without a woman behind you, pushing you on."

When I saw what it was, I tore it into bits, opened the window and scattered the pieces to the wind.

Looking at them flying away, my mind full with my memories of her, I'd no intention of ever being with anyone else. Rachel was my childhood sweetheart. From our very first "date" we'd both known there would be no other for either of us, and in my grief all I wanted was to spend the rest of my life on my own.

She was special.

So very special.

No one could ever replace her…

And so it was that four years passed.

Until Carys decided it was time to "push me on".

But when she did, I fell in a big way.

In a way that, four years earlier, I thought I would never, *ever*, fall again.

Yet if I hadn't, Abigail might not have been born.

That's how strange life often is.

One thing leading to another.

When they happen, are they coincidences?

Or are they meant to be?

It all started one evening as I was watching *Sleepless in Seattle* for the umpteenth time. It was one of my favourite films, and I'd just reached that weepy part where, after years of heartache for his wife after her early death from cancer, Tom Hanks' "Sam", and Meg Ryan's "Annie", lock eyes for the first time across a busy road, but neither is able say anything except "Hello," when Carys entered the room, switched off the dvd without so much as a "do you mind?" and said, 'Daddy, you've got to shake yourself out of this and find someone to go places with. You can't keep going out all on your own.'

("going out" being the gym, or swimming, or playing golf – especially golf, but no partner, just me playing against the course, as I did then, preferring my own company.)

'I prefer my own company, Carys. Gives me time to think.'

'You mean *brood*, Dad. Mummy knew you would and told me to make sure you didn't. That's why she wrote that list for you. She *wanted* you to marry again.'

'Don't go on about it, sweetheart,' I protested. 'I'm okay as I am.'

But it was like water off a duck's back. When she chose to be, Carys could be as determined as her mum. And she'd no intention of giving in.

'It's been *four* years, Dad,' she insisted. 'You've got more than half your life still ahead of you. It's time you found someone. What about Meryn? Remember? I introduced you to her in the Ddraig Goch. She was at the next table with her friend, Gaenor. She's a really lovely person, Meryn, exactly right for you. You have the same interests – including the theatre. And you both love travelling. Now that she's on her own again, just like you, why don't you ask her out for a meal, or something?'

Carys – I said to myself – you don't know it, but ever since meeting her I've thought of little else. But like Tom Hanks' "Sam", I was unable to say anything more to her than, "Hello". She looked so exquisite, just like porcelain is exquisite, beautifully dressed, immaculately so, the most gorgeous green eyes, and slim with short, fair hair, that I was tongue-tied, not something I'm normally prone to. Since then, every time I saw her in town, my next few days – and nights – were spent dreaming wild dreams about her.

'She's far too young for me, Cara.' (ten years) 'Besides, with her looks, and everything else she's got going for her, she'll be swamped with invitations. I wouldn't have the courage to ask her.'

'Oh, Dad, don't be silly,' Carys said. 'The worst she can say is no. But she might say yes. Except you'll never know without asking her.'

Which, as these things happen, turned out to be true, for the very next day I bumped into her in Marks & Sparks Food Department. Not quite the top of the Empire State Building where Tom's "Sam" and Meg's "Annie" get to hold hands for the first time, and shooting stars burst across the sky, but I wasn't complaining. After some nervous hesitation on my part I asked her out for a meal. And after some similar nervous hesitation on Meryn's part, she accepted.

And that was that, as they say.

All of which brings me to the day I first met Carys's new beau and the first of my digressions, being that my letter is to a five-year old Abigail, but won't be read by her for another twelve, maybe fourteen more years. So, rather like a tapestry needs a canvas and coloured threads to create a whole picture, I'll need to pause every now and then to explain things to her, for her to know and understand all that happened. And just like a tapestry, my letter and chapters are interwoven together to make my telling of the story whole.

The end of one blurs into the start of the other, and there's no other way to write it.

But there again, this – for most of us I suspect – is part of the pattern of life.

Tears are not always tears of sorrow, but can also be tears of laughter. And smiles are not always smiles of joy, but can also be sad smiles.

Certainly, I'm no exception to this.

Blurred edges.

- three -

But before telling you about Mummy's new beau — who, as you'll probably have guessed, was your Daddy, Abigail — you're likely wondering why I'm telling you all this, of all that happened before you were even born.

Well, among other things, I want you to know we were once a happy family, just like any other close family, normal, despite our traits, and united, looking forward to many happy years together — not knowing of the events that were yet to come. To use an analogy here, Abigail, a little like looking at a full moon, seeing but its bright side hovering above us, yet all the time it has a dark side too, that we can't see. But it's there. Oh yes, despite not being able to see it, it's there, looming like a dark shadow over us, waiting to show its face.

But back then we didn't *know* it was there, and life was as I'm telling it to you now, and brings me back to that day — how well I remember it — of how I came to first meet your Daddy.

It was early evening and I was taking Meryn out to dinner.

Even though you won't remember Meryn, or the pretty dresses she once loved to buy you, she plays a big part in my telling you this story, because if it wasn't for Meryn, little sixpence, Mummy and Daddy might never have married.

And as I've already said, you might never have been born.

That, to repeat, is how strange life often is.

One thing leading to another.

And then another.

Just like the proverbial rhyme my mother's youngest brother, Uncle Billy, taught me when I was a child (he was great, Uncle Billy, you'd have loved him) to impress on me how even the smallest of decisions you make, can only too often have a knock-on effect on events that might one day shape the rest of your life. Uncle Billy also told me that the moral of this rhyme has been around six hundred years, so there must be some truth in it, having stood such a test of time.

It goes something like this.

For want of a nail the shoe was lost.
For want of a shoe the horse was lost.
For want of a horse the rider was lost.
For want of a rider the message was lost.
For want of a message the battle was lost.
For want of a battle the kingdom was lost.
All for the want of a nail.

It certainly was true that day with Meryn.

Because all I was doing was driving her to *Plas-ar-Hendir* (it means "hall on ancient land") now converted to an ivy-clad country house hotel, very grand – I was still at the stage of trying to impress her. I'd known her only three weeks, we'd not exchanged a cross word and I was already smitten by her, when…

'Damn,' I exclaimed.

'What's the matter?' she asked, startled.

'I've left my wallet at home, in my other suit.'

She settled back into her seat. 'Is *that* all? For a moment, I thought the world was coming to an end. Turn back, we've plenty of time.'

And that's what we did. Turned back.

For a wallet – an ordinary, everyday, wallet.

But which turned out to be my proverbial "nail".

And so it was that some ten minutes later we drove in through the house gates and up the drive, and there, parked outside the front door, I saw this red clapped-out-looking VW Beetle.

I didn't have to guess twice at its owner.

I'd realised for some time that there was someone new in Carys's life. The extra time taken to pretty herself up before going out to "nowhere special, only to Anna's," (her best friend). There were also the phone calls with Carys always the first to grab it – a cordless, invariably resting on her chair arm lately, as we sat and chatted, or read, or watched TV. Eyes lighting up, cheeks flushing, she'd say 'Hi!' (but giving no name) then drift out of the room to continue the conversation in some other part of the house, out of my earshot. Minutes later, she'd rush up the stairs with an accompanying shout, 'I've left the phone on the settle, Dad,' and giving me no chance to ask: 'Who was it, Cara?'

Nor again, moments later, when there's similar rush back down the stairs and a 'Bye, Dad, don't wait up, I may be late,' – "may" is now her new word for "will". The front door slams, then the car door, the engine vroom-vrooms – an overpowered Mini Cooper with wide wheels – and she's tyre-screeching off down the drive.

What's more, I'd quickly come to realise that this one was different. Carys was normally as open as a book, secrecy wasn't part of her nature, but whoever, whatever this one was, she was going out way of her way to keep him to herself. Realising she must have a reason for this, I'd not questioned her. But now, at last, I had the chance to meet him…

I could have driven away, of course, but on the other hand I needed that damned wallet.

Ignoring Meryn's restraining hand on my arm, and her: 'Wait a sec, Luke, before you go rushing in–' I got out of the car, strolled to the front door, fumbled the Yale key in the lock, took my time opening it, entered, called out, 'It's only me, Cara', went upstairs for the fateful wallet, searched for it (even though I knew where it was), found it, and finally went back down and entered the family den.

They were sitting in separate chairs, chatting all innocent-like across the room. But I wasn't fooled. Carys's face was flushed; what's more she knew it was, and tried to pass it all off with a casual, almost laid-back greeting.

'Daddy, I'd like you to meet Ian.'

"Pimpernel" got to his feet and at last I realised why all the secrecy about him. This was no suited suitor with matching tie that Rachel would have approved of I was being introduced to. Other than his height (six one?) and the colour of his hair (dark) this was a James Dean type: brown-leather bomber jacket, white crew-neck tee-shirt, trainers, narrow blue jeans. Even more disconcerting, he was much younger than Carys's twenty-six years – five, maybe even six years younger.

'Hello, Ian,' I said, offering him my hand.

But thinking: 'Carys, for goodness sake, what are you playing at?'

And wondering what Rachel would have done if it was she, and not me, meeting him...

- four -

In saying I wondered what Gammy Rachel would have done, Abigail, it's just that but days before she died, she got me to promise to take especial care of your Mummy Carys, and give every new boyfriend the same third degree she'd have given him.

When she asked it, I was holding her, frail in my arms.

And looking down at her still-to-me beautiful face.

Forty-five, I thought.

Rachel, oh Rachel.

You're too young to die.

Nevertheless, I made her the promise…

So, it would have been the same had it been Tom, Bob or Harry standing there, Abigail, not your Daddy.

As I let go of the leather-jacketed young man's hand, standing there looking nervous, Rachel and her propensity to instant decisions, seeing everything in either black or white but never in between, was making it hard for me to know what to do.

Especially as I could guess that *whatever* she'd have done (tactics-wise that is – or not done come to that, Rachel was a virtuoso of the pregnant silence) it would, after an instant appraisal (and most likely one of her silences) have resulted in his early and discomfited departure.

Carys sensed my conflict and guessed my reason, she knew her mum well, too. Taking hold of Ian's arm to let me know he was already special to her, warning me with those flashing eyes of hers (my, I thought, just like Rachel) not to say anything to make her choose or I might end up the loser, her next gambit was to sit down, pulling Ian down beside her on the sofa and snuggling up to him.

Okay, Cara, I get the message.

There's something about daughters, especially where fathers are concerned. After Rachel died, Carys told me she was going to change her image. As Rachel's recipe for good health (for us, not for herself, and no escape, apart from gastroenteritis that is, and even then only if backed up by a doctor's note) had been three square meals a day, plus a hearty supper to go to bed on, I didn't think it was a bad idea.

Within months, at 5'6", two stone lighter at just eight stone, her skin golden tanned, her hair considerably shortened from the Raphaelite style that Rachel loved half way down her back, its tawny colour highlighted, she looked stunning. I was likely to be prejudiced, of course, but she really did.

But even when daughters reach twenty-six – and are free-spirited (as Carys most definitely was) – fathers still feel protective about them, and should a daughter wish to marry – and by this I mean *really* want to – it's an absolute must for her chosen to be Sir Galahad *and* Sir Lancelot all rolled into one. But this Ian of Carys's didn't appear to remotely fill this criteria. Anything but, being honest.

And so, as I was standing there conflicting over what Rachel would have done if it was she – and not me – meeting him, Meryn came to my rescue, calling out, 'It's just me,' as she opened the front door.

'We're in here, Meryn,' I replied – unnecessarily, but it helped break the impasse.

Although she was a few years younger than me, in the brief time I'd known her, Meryn had already shown she had a "wise head" on her slender shoulders, one that coolly weighed things up – the opposite of Rachel – rather than being carried away by sudden impulse or by sentiment, and I'd rapidly come to come to respect her judgement.

Entering the room she sensed the atmosphere and tried to defuse the situation, giving Carys a hug and a kiss on the cheek, 'Hello, Carys.' And then turned to Ian, and said. 'How's the car racing coming along, Ian?'

Hey! What was this? Meryn not only knew about Ian, she'd clearly *met* him as well, yet she'd not said a word to me, not even hinted. This must have been what she wanted to tell me minutes ago when I was getting out of the car. What was going on here? Some sort of conspiracy to keep it all from ogre father?

And what was this about car racing?

I interrupted the mutual greetings. 'You're into car racing, Ian? In what way? Mechanic?'

He gave Carys a questioning glance and I saw her return him an "It's okay" with those eyes of hers again.

'Stock cars,' he said. 'I race them. And if I can find a sponsor, hope to eventually move up to Formula One.'

I dropped on to the other settee, pulling at Meryn's skirt for her to sit next to me.

We weren't going anywhere, not until I knew more.

Three hours later and dinner over, I was still discussing it with Meryn over coffee around a log fire in *Plas-ar-Hendir's* lounge.

All due to my proverbial "because of a wallet".

Uncle Billy, you never said a truer word. If I'd not forgotten the blessed thing, I wouldn't have met Ian, Meryn and I wouldn't be having this conversation, and what happened next might never have happened.

But after hearing all I needed to hear from Ian, we left him and Carys together at home. He looking all shell-shocked by the grilling, and she fussing over him while giving me the kind of glares only a daughter, not even a wife, can get away with.

Over dinner I told Meryn about my promise to Rachel, and what I thought she would have done...

Meryn thought the opposite.

'A stock car driver,' I protested. 'Rachel would have had a fit. As for racing Formula One cars? In his dreams. And that's as far as he'll get.'

'But he's good,' Meryn repeated, still taking Carys's side. 'He can turn his Beetle around on a sixpence.'

'From what I saw of it, it looks like he's raced in it. And come off worst. As for the gap between stock cars and grand prix, it's as wide as the Grand Canyon.'

'He's only twenty-one, Luke. He's got plenty of time.'

'No, he hasn't. I knew someone else with the same ambition when *he* was only twenty-one, too, but already in a different league to any other driver I ever knew, and way above a bumping car driver like Ian. He also had a wealthy father backing him, but he still had to grind it out on the Formula Three and Two circuits first, before making it.'

'Ian's hoping to find a sponsor.'

'Except, stock car racing's not where they go looking for talent. And even if they did, he's not yet won a race. But okay, say he *does* find one, what's in front of him? Years of constantly on the move from one European track to another, living in third or fourth-hand motorhomes and eating takeaway meals. What kind of a life would that be for Carys?'

'An exciting one?'

'Oh, come on, Meryn! Would *you* like it?'

'Maybe not, but Carys is still young enough to–'

'She's twenty-six, not twenty-one like Ian. At that age he's too young to know his own mind. What if he met someone younger along the way? I don't want Carys getting hurt.'

Meryn's eyes opened theatrically wide. 'Too young? Weren't you and Rachel only seventeen when you first went out?' She paused. 'I think you're forgetting, Luke, that Carys is no longer a child. You can't tell her what to do any more, those days are long gone, all you can do is advise. And even here you should tread carefully or you'll end up making her all the more determined. As for the gap in their ages, there are a few years between us, don't forget.'

'That's different, Meryn. We're both mature enough to know our own minds. As for Rachel and me, I was going to be a dull accountant, all solid and dependable with a secure income, not some stock car driver.'

Another objection struck me. 'He doesn't even have a job. Part-times as a hotel waiter.'

'To pay for his racing. All the more credit to him.'

I changed tack. 'Okay, so what about–'

'Sorry, Luke,' Meryn cut across me, 'I'm on Carys's side. And you can hardly blame her for going out with him. Tall, dark and handsome as they say. Besides, it's early days yet—'

'But I still know hardly anything about him.'

'Then give yourself a chance to find out. As for Carys, she tells me she's having a great time and really enjoying Ian's company.'

'You're not just saying that?'

'Luke, you should know me better than that by now.'

'Okay, but there's still the age gap'

This was my biggest concern.

'Not that again!' Meryn protested.

'But it can't be avoided, Meryn. Carys has always dreamed of having children, so don't forget what happened this time last year, when she was found to have ovarian cysts and had to have them removed. And the fear it caused, which is still with us, despite them being benign, what with her family history on Rachel's side.'

I paused before stressing the facts.

'Rachel was only forty-five. Her sister, Helen, was even younger, thirty-nine. And their father – with him it was stomach cancer – he was just forty-one. As for *his* mother, *Nain* Bellis (the Welsh word for grandmother, Abigail, pronounced "nine") she was only thirty-two. That's why the surgeon advised Carys to have a hysterectomy at thirty, kids or no kids – that gives her just four years. But with Ian only twenty-one and an uncertain future, well…What's more, to be fair to him, he should be told the risk.'

'Luke,' Meryn said, I sensed she was tiring of the argument. 'It's for Carys and her doctor to decide when she should have the op. All you can do is be there for her. As for Ian, it's early days yet, nothing may come of it. But if it does, it's for Carys to tell him her fears, not you.'

She lightened her tone. 'So, why don't you pull back from it and see how things work out? If it's to be, it's to be. And knowing how Carys can dig her heels in when she wants, I doubt there's anything you can do to change it anyway. Nor should you try.'

She slid her cup across the table. 'And I'd like another coffee, mine's gone cold.'

- five -

And that, Abigail, was how I first met your Daddy.

Mummy wasn't being devious in not telling me about him.
It's simply that she knew I was somewhat protective (well,
maybe a touch over-protective). Also, that Gammy Rachel
had made me make that promise. So, perhaps she was just a
little wary of testing me on it with someone so different to
previous boyfriends.

But as for my trying to honour it, it wasn't Daddy himself
that was my problem. In fact, in the weeks following our little
chat (okay, interrogation) I quickly got to know him and liked
him a lot. Nor was I swayed one way or the other by his style
of clothes – but there again I'd no choice in this. Mummy
would have shot me down in flames if I'd dared comment,
I'd worn the same style myself when I was young and she'd
seen photos of me, but with jeans worn even tighter then,
dressing "properly" to quote my mam (your *Hennain*, Abigail
– "old Nain", Welsh for "great grandmother") only when I
had to.

Nor was I, in truth, against Mummy going out with Daddy
as such, I wasn't in any way a killjoy. Nor would Gammy
Rachel have been, come to that. A beautiful pianist who
played Beethoven like a dream, she loved pop music, too –
especially jive. If I close my eyes I can see her still, her black
hair bouncing, 21-inch waisted, flared skirt (the style of those

times) swirling around her, her face alight with the joy of it all as we danced away to one of the then big bands.

Carys, too, after she won me around. Watching her and Ian dance together when Meryn and I went with them to a "New Year", or similar party, both in perfect harmony, would have delighted even Terpsichore – a modern day Terpsichore that is, playing a guitar instead of a lyre, and wearing Suzi Quatro leathers instead of a flimsy white Greek gown.

Carys.

Rachel.

Both so full of life.

It's still hard to accept that they're–

But I've digressed again, Abigail, which as you know by now is me to a proverbial "T".

I was saying, wasn't I, about trying to honour my promise to Gammy and going to add that neither was it your Daddy's car-racing dream I objected to – we're all entitled to dreams – nor, so I thought at the time, was I allowing myself to be influenced by the extra dangers he would be facing a the hoped-not event they came true. I'd had my own share of danger, serving my two years national service in Malaya with a Welsh Fusiliers regiment (bullets coming too close to me a couple of times, like the one that so suddenly, and so disbelievingly, took my squad pal Jimmy Jones, crouching next to me) and no one should expect to go through life wrapped up in cotton wool.

Except, looking back on it now, although I'd only just met him, maybe I *was* concerned for him after all. If anything goes wrong in dreams, it's gone when we wake up. But in real life we're not so in control. The other hopeful young racing driver I knew was Piers Courage, who became one of the top aces of his time. Like me, he was studying accountancy (that's how I met him) to go into his family's brewery business, but he gave it up to follow *his* dream…and was killed (only 28) at the Dutch Grand Prix in Zandvoort, when he slid wide at a sharp corner, ran up a bank and crashed. I was watching it, horrified, on tv, as his car rolled over and over, then finished upright and burst into flames – with Piers trapped inside, sitting at his wheel. He didn't stand a chance.

So, yes, when Daddy first told me his ambition I did have a flash of seeing it again, Piers engulfed by fire and, I confess, would have done anything to have changed his dream. For his sake…and for Carys's, too, for her never to have to be the one left grieving.

I was also unhappy, putting it mildly, about the lack of financial stability his chosen path had to offer her. Mummy was a PA to the CEO of a large Mutual Assurance company (and well paid) and even though I didn't think she had any special right to a life paved with gold, she was my daughter, we were (in her words) "the bestest of pals", and I didn't want to see her dragged down a broken dirt road either.

But my biggest concern was still the age difference. Twenty years on, Daddy's forty-one years wouldn't sound so bad against Mummy's forty-six, but the gap between his twenty-one and her twenty-six, seemed huge. To my mind (no offence to Daddy) it was a grown woman going out with a young man only a few years out of school. Yes, I know that

Gammy and I were only seventeen when we first started going out together, and yes, alright, so we were. But we were both the same age, and that, to me, made it all very different.

I know it sounds unreasonable of me, Abigail, and maybe it was. But for you to understand *why* I was so protective, we have to go back to the day Mummy Carys was born.

To when I was holding her in my arms for the very first time—

Oh dear, Abigail, tears in my eyes.

Just give me a moment…

Okay, Abigail, tears over and continuing from where I left off…

Carys is a Welsh name, sixpence. Chosen by Rachel, it means "love". And throughout her all too-brief life, Mummy-in-Heaven was all of that. In one person.

One minute old, she'd been given to me to nurse as Rachel's life was being battled for by the doctor and midwife in the bedroom above us. If only Rachel could see her, touch her, I can remember myself thinking as I cwched my precious bundle, making her feel safe and secure, it would help her to fight.

Meantime, as Carys slept there snuggled in my arms, looking so tiny and trusting, I made a vow that no harm would ever come to her, not if I could help it.

She was such a beautiful baby, neither red or wrinkled, but well-padded and olive-skinned – as was Ewen, their colouring inherited from Rachel. She didn't murmur as I washed her on my towelled lap with cotton wool dipped in warm water,

29

gently dried her, and wrapped her in a fluffy white shawl I had airing in front of the fire, then gave her a drink of warm boiled water. She opened her eyes and looked at me as if she already knew me and gave me a smile (it was definitely a smile, not a twitch) then fell fast asleep as I nursed her, at the same time listening to the commotion going on in the room above us and praying for Rachel's life to be saved.

That time, my prayers were answered. Or maybe Rachel was praying too, and it was hers God heard. I was then allowed to take Carys up to her to hold for a brief moment, before being ushered out of the room for her to get some much needed sleep, and for me to phone my mum, who was looking after Ewen, to tell her that (after having had two tearaway sons) she had the granddaughter she'd always dreamt of, and to bring Ewen home to meet his little sister.

I can still remember the look of…well, almost of awe on his three year old face as he peeped at Carys, now wide-eyed and still shawled in my arms. Until then, he'd enjoyed all our attention and we were worried he'd maybe be jealous now he was going to have to share it.

'Is she my new baby fister?' he questioned as if hardly able to believe it, and as I answered 'yes,' Carys yawned and screwed up her face.

'She's tired,' he told me. 'Shall we make her a puc of tea?'

For Ewen, even at that tender age, a "puc of tea" was the great cure-all.

'Maybe later,' I replied. 'Just give her your little finger to hold.'

He did, very tentatively. Carys grasped it tight, and from that moment he was her protector (though he'd never openly reveal such *"cissy"* feelings, not even as a small child).

But as he stood there in awe of his "baby fister", with Carys still gripping his finger, and my mother aching to hold her ('In a minute', I thought, not wanting to let her go) little did I realise how much my promise that no harm would ever come to her meant. That although Rachel's will to live brought her through that day, she would never be really well again, and I would have so much to do with the precious bundle in my arms, all the getting-up-in-the-nights to feed her; the teething; the many sleepless nights when she caught the usual ailments (every ruddy one of them, it seemed to me then, except maybe verrucas).

And the funny side of her growing up, too.

Doing my best to keep a straight face when she used to dress up in in Rachel's clothes, best wedding hat flopped down over her face, stylish coat in folds swamping her four year old frame as she tottered on stiletto heels, handbag on her arm, calling herself "Mrs Rees" and telling me, very serious, about her accountant husband and her two small children, a boy and a girl.

But it was all this that had created the special bond between us.

And would always be there.

No matter what.

Whatever her age.

And all it entailed.

Including that dim-brained eye consultant who told us (Carys was also in the room, hearing this) that she'd be blind by the time she was fifteen. She burst into tears, as any ten year old would. It turned out he was wrong. But it gave us all a hellish week before a Harley Street doctor was able to reassure us that an operation would correct the problem. It was a success, followed by tears of joy this time, not just Carys's, but Rachel's and mine too (and *whisper* it, Ewen's as well) when the bandages were removed and Carys could see everything clearly again.

That evening, as a treat for Carys, we took her to the theatre to see *The Mousetrap* (a play by her then favourite author, Agatha Christie, she must have read every one of her books). We managed to get seats in the second row of the stalls, and at a crucial point when an actor enters a room (supposedly unaware the killer is hiding behind the door waiting for him) an enthralled Carys, able now to see everything clearly, shouted out for all the theatre to hear:

'Look out, he's behind the door!'

The actor came to the edge of the stage, smiled down at Carys and said:

'Thank you, young lady. But let's pretend I never heard your warning.'

He returned to the scene with Carys ignoring all the faces turned around to smile at her and tossing her head aside – but Ewen (*whisper this, too*) then a self-conscious thirteen year-old, ducked down behind the seat in front of him, his face all red, poor boy.

Which in essence epitomised their different natures. Brooding about this, I opened a pine chest of drawers and pulled out an album of them both, taken when Carys was nine and Ewen twelve, and browsed through it, thinking back to when they were taken and how what happened that day evinced this.

Rachel had engaged a photographer to come to the house to take various shots of them, intending to have the best of each framed. Straight after breakfast, Carys was already trying on dresses in front of her bedroom mirror, finally deciding on a full length Empire-line party dress with lace collar and cuffs – mostly brown, to tone in with her tawny hair – whereas Ewen hid in the attic until it was too late to change out of his already muddied and torn jeans and T-shirt into neater clothes, only to be dragged to his fate protesting, "I don't want to do any *cissy* pictures."

For all that, the resulting shots were terrific. I looked at the two Rachel chose to be framed, hanging up side by side on the wall, and couldn't help but smile. Ewen had had his last say in the pose he was made to assume, studiously reading a book – its title, *Great Expectations,* on the front cover, clearly showing he's holding it upside down.

As for the portraits, apart from one being a boy – very definitely a *boy*, a veritable *tinker* of a boy, with the most mischievous brown eyes and infectious grin – and the other just as definitely a girl, in every sense of the word including two of the cutest dimples – they were as alike as two peas in a pod…

Reminding me again how close they both were, right up to the end.

And when it came there was no one more cut up than Ewen, though not for anyone to see, but bottled up, grieving deep inside himself…and still does, the many times he talks about her, and the wistful tone you can hear in his voice.

But I'm getting ahead of myself now, Abigail, instead of my usual digressing.

So, returning to the promise I made to Rachel, I still didn't want to see Mummy throw her life away, chasing someone else's nebulous car-racing dream across Europe, wondering where the next penny was coming from.

Nevertheless, after listening to Meryn's advice over coffee at Plas-ar-Hendir that evening, when I got back home, the house was in darkness. Mummy and Daddy – no doubt to avoid any further interrogation – had escaped somewhere out of my way.

And so I went straight to bed.

Brooded over all that Meryn had said.

Came to the conclusion she was right.

And decided to let matters take their course.

- six -

Six months went by.

Anna, Carys's best friend, was married yesterday. She looked beautiful.

As did Carys in her bridesmaid's dress.

Looking (prophetically?) like a bride herself.

But today, back to wearing narrow-leg jeans and polo-necked jumper, she and Ian had gone for a walk along the beach, both talking earnestly about something.

And I was sitting at my desk editing my second novel, and gazing through the window.

A couple of years before Rachel died, I turned to writing, a sort of hark-back I suppose, to when I'd wanted to read English at university – instead of being an accountant, at my father's dictatorial insistence and joining his practice. But when he retired on a good pension, I sold it and started on my first novel – *The Illuminati Conspiracy*. Though not the bestseller I'd hoped for when it came out last year, it was still well received, with good reviews and none bad.

But I was hoping to make it with my second historical, solving in factional form the famous *Mary Celeste* sea mystery, giving the kudos of my research to a fictional hero and heroine. And should it do well, maybe the *Illuminati* paperback would get a publicity boost because of it.

Who knew…

There was no harm dreaming.

Always better to keep looking on the bright side.

Time enough for disappointment when it actually happens.

But today my mind had wandered on to other things, uppermost being how to find time to spring a surprise on Meryn and take her on holiday. I was thinking Sorrento – separate rooms – which isn't to say I don't have blood in my veins, I do, but I was still old-fashioned that way.

Also, Meryn was so…well, "flawless" is the word that first springs to mind – although it's not the one I'm searching for – especially as her deep, green eyes when holding mine, always conveyed *so* much – but I also knew she wouldn't agree to one room, well, not so soon at least.

Yet that aside, Meryn was the one, my *"Sleepless in Seattle"*, and where better than Sorrento to make a time-honoured, romantic proposal – with the romantic sweep of the Bay of Naples as a backdrop?

Meantime (and as we both knew her answer) she'd told me she wanted to start our new life together in a new home, so the house was up for sale. It made sense, I suppose, especially with it being so full of my memories. But with the property market having hit a new low recently, it was another reason for my having delayed Sorrento until now – I didn't want to miss any chance of a sale. Still, the thought of us spending time alone together in the sun was getting stronger by the day, and I couldn't put it off any longer.

But I was going to miss this old place. Spacious, yet with a cosy atmosphere that made it a warm family home, especially with all its antiques, some handed down hundreds of years from Rachel's ancestors – the Welsh dresser with its blue willow plates, the settle nestled next to the moon-faced grandfather clock tick-tocking away in the hall – all ingrained with generations of loving polish and invested with their dreams – others so carefully bought by Rachel during our years together: the *ford gron* (round table), paintings – oils and water colours – and china, how Rachel loved china: Dresden, Meissen, Staffordshire figures dotted all around the house (every time she saw a piece she fancied in an antique shop it was pointless trying to persuade her we already had enough), and a baby grand piano I bought her on her thirtieth birthday…

I arranged for it to be smuggled into the house while she was out shopping and all the subterfuge was well worth it, seeing her look of surprise turning to one of excitement when she returned home and saw it through the drawing room window, then ran in, dumped her shopping in the front hall, shot straight into the room and began playing it. Dinner was late that evening.

But Meryn was more for modern furniture than antique, and this meant they would all shortly – and sooner than expected – be divided between Ewen and Carys, and then passed on to *their* children and other generations to come.

Apart from the piano, that is, which Meryn also loved to play. She was as gifted a pianist as Rachel, with a touch so sensitive her fingers seemed to float over the keys. Again, like Rachel, her favourite composer was Beethoven – I loved to listen to her playing him and seeing her face lost in the beauty of his music.

Yet, I was going to miss my things. It was as if they were a part of me. As for the old place, I was going to miss it, too. It was so conducive for writing. Fine weather or storm the view from my study window was breath-taking. I could gaze across the bay to the Isle of Anglesey and the Irish sea beyond, and by swivelling my chair see the Conwy estuary and the crenelated medieval castle standing on its far bank, still guarding the approaches to the mountains of Snowdonia and also see Carys and Ian coming up the drive from their stroll along the beach.

Neither could see me because of the sun reflecting off my window panes.

It was a glorious spring day, the sun was shining out of a clear blue sky, glistening on the waters as far as the horizon, and the mountains were still topped white with snow. It felt good just being alive yet, at the same time, sad that Rachel wasn't with me to enjoy it.

As they came nearer, still talking earnestly, Carys gripped Ian's arm, impressing whatever it was on him, and he nodded back in reply. I had a feeling I was going to be asked something important and could guess what it was going to be.

My answer would be "yes" – on condition.

But Meryn was right. "If it's to be, it's to be."

Ian and I were now good friends, as good a friend as any man can be with someone clearly bent on marrying his one-in-a-million daughter. We often played snooker together, Ian's pastime at which he excelled – if it can be construed that me striking off, Ian recording a break of "fifty" or more, me hitting one more "red", and him clearing up, counts as me participating.

However, this snooker side of our relationship sometimes bothered me a little.

It may, of course, be my imagination, but it seemed to me that in always wiping me off the table, Ian was maybe, just maybe, being *too* competitive, as if he was trying to show Carys – who recorded our scores for us – that her Dad wasn't quite so great, after all.

His shots never rolled in, they almost demolished the pockets.

Bang! A red slammed in. *Bang!* A black.

Bang! Another red. *Bang!* Another black.

Added to that, Ian can, on occasions, switch into a sudden dark mood. Carys has noticed it, too and playfully calls him "my Heathcliff", the anti-hero from *Wuthering Heights*, another of her favourite books – but as I've said, it sometimes bothers me.

Bang! (and I mean ***Bang!***) Another red. *Bang!* Another black.

And when he calls out to Carys to record his break on the board…

'That's fifty-six, Cris… (Ian's own name for Carys) …What's your father's score?'

'Nothing so far. But my Dad's game's golf, not snooker.'

…it seems to me there's too much of an exultant tone in his voice, and maybe his victorious smile is not all to do with winning the frame.

But perhaps I'm mistaken?

Whatever, as a result of my paying for him to test drive a Formula 1 type racing car around Oulton Park in nearby Cheshire, he'd realised – with *no* persuasion from *anyone* – that as good a driver as he undoubtedly was (and he *was* good, Carys and I went with him to cheer him on and he scorched around the track) he didn't possess that extra something all top drivers have to make it in Formula 1. So, he now worked for the Forestry Commission, happy in his job, still racing stock cars and thinking of moving up to car rallying. (If so, I'd be behind him all the way, even be his navigator if he wanted; I knew how to read maps from my time in the army.)

How wrong could I have been in my first impression him? *Thanks Meryn.*

Yet I should have known it from my own experience. Looking back again to my army days I can recollect being told by Jimmy (the one who got killed out in Malaya) that his first impression of me was of something of a rebel, what with the brown leather zipper jacket, white tee-shirt and jeans I was wearing when we met on our first day in the training barracks, before being issued with our nondescript khaki drill kits.

No wonder Rachel's mother was so set against me at first. And following on from that, maybe *my* reaction on first meeting Ian was seeing something of myself in him, remembering what I'd been like at the same age?

Strange how life parallels itself.

Now the whole process was being repeated with Carys and Ian. Except Rachel's mother had wanted us to wait a few years, and "*save up to have some money behind you.*"

My father had also thought the same.

But Rachel and I didn't listen and married at twenty-one.

And because we'd been so happy, proving we'd been right, *my* advice to Ian and Carys was going to be along the same lines – but none of them, I hoped, selfish.

Okay, I accept that the threat to Carys – the inherent gene on Rachel's side of her family – was never very far from my mind. Or from Carys's either. Nor could we bury our heads in the sands, pretending the threat wasn't there. It was real. Very real. So much so, we talked about it a lot after Rachel died and told our GP of our fears – but when he dismissed them we wrote to The Royal Marsden Hospital in London, one of the top, if not *the* top cancer hospital in the country, giving them Carys's family history and asking their advice.

It's a sad reflection of our then National Health Service, but at that time only The Marsden had ovarian scanning facilities. And even though it appears – from what we're told – that cancer screening and treatment is much improved today, it seems to me from what I read and hear, that there are still far too many cases of neglect, even in this day, in heeding to patients' first signs of their symptoms – and then misdiagnosis – until eventually being referred to hospital, only to be faced by more delay, often stretching into months, before being given an appointment with a consultant, followed by more waits because of a continued shortage of equipment, and finally starting tests (but often, too late) and getting the right treatment – which even then is denied in some parts of the country because of the cost of new drugs (or living on the wrong postal code side of a street) – thereby still putting people's lives at risk. The same old form of neglect that demands to be bettered as much today as it did years back.

But in The Marsden's case we received a reply almost by return of post, inviting Carys to London for tests, which confirmed she was high risk. As a result, she was put on an immediate monitoring program, with screening every six months.

It was this that told us she had ovarian cysts.

Thankfully, the operation to remove them showed them to be benign. But it rang the warning bells even louder. And ever since then, although Carys rarely mentioned it – as if by not doing so it would go away – I knew it was there in the back of her mind. And in mine, too, it never left me. With her twenty-seventh birthday now but five months away, there was only three and a bit years to when she'd been advised to have a hysterectomy, and we were both conscious of the clock ticking away, with the awareness of it hanging over us like some sort of nebulous shadow.

But as Carys and Ian reached my study window, the clock running out was not my reason for the advice I was going to offer.

Nor was it going to have to wait long, because Carys could now see me.

Tapping on the window, she called up through the open transom. 'Daddy...' bless her, she sounded nervous, 'may we come through? Ian's got something he wants to ask you.'

Ian looked even edgier. A rare happening, he'd become so confident lately (not that he wasn't before, but he was now even more so) and mature, way past his twenty one years –

not just in work, but in everything and with everyone – I was tempted, sorely tempted, to play the stern parent role and get my own back for all those snooker wipe-outs.

Except that would be mean, I thought, wrestling the urge.

Come on, Luke, remember having to ask Rachel's mother, and what a terrifying experience that was. Be kind to the boy and put him out of his misery.

'Of course,' I replied, 'and bring that bottle of bubbly with you, Carys. The one I said I was keeping for a special occasion.'

Her face lit up. Yanking Ian almost off his feet, she raced to the front door.

Oh, Cara!

I can still see you now, the way your eyes shone, you were that excited.

'Have you talked it over with your mother and father, Ian?'

This was important to me, because over recent months, Meryn and I had gone out for the occasional meal with Anne and Tony, Ian's parents. Not only did we get on well, but we'd all four realised for some time that this moment was inevitable – the only question was "when?". Yet what I was about to suggest might not get their full blessing. At least, not for another year or so.

Sitting alongside Carys on the sofa opposite me, Ian replied. 'I've hinted at it, Luke, but I thought I should ask you first.'

Ian called me by my first name, we'd long dispensed with any old-fashioned "Mr Rees" politeness. I'd always had to call Rachel's mother "Mrs Bellis". Only if Ewen or Carys were with us was I allowed to call her anything other than that – and that was only "Gran".

'Cris has told me her family history,' Ian continued. 'I can understand her being concerned about it, but I've told her it makes no difference to how I feel about her.'

Carys clutched his arm. There were tears in her eyes. I could feel some in mine, too.

'Thanks, Ian.' Coughing to clear my throat, it took me a moment to continue. 'In which case, I just happen to know your Mum and Dad are going to be as pleased about it as I am…'

They turned to each other, looking so relieved, goodness only knows what they thought was going to be my response.

'…except I have one condition…'

Their faces dropped as they wondered what I was about to impose.

'…or maybe "suggestion" would be a better word.'

I paused to wonder whether I was giving them the right advice.

I thought I was.

No, I was sure I was.

At the time.

'I'm not much for a lengthy engagement, until Ian's earning more – no, hear me out, Carys, just for once.'

Carys subsided back into her cushions, which wasn't exactly her nature, there was a lot of Rachel in her.

'With the house market slow at the moment, there are any number of bargains about. While you're waiting to build up some money behind you, if prices suddenly shoot up again you could find yourselves worse off. So, if you're sure about each other, absolutely sure, my advice is to buy now…' I hesitated, '…and maybe think about moving the wedding forward?'

Something in their shared glances told me they'd been considering the same thing, and so, feeling less like I was inflicting my own views on them, I continued.

'But should you decide to wait, then at least consider getting on the property ladder now, and maybe let the place out in the meantime. Talk it over with your parents, Ian, and if they're happy with it, I'll help you with the deposit. And should you see the ideal place and decide to live in it yourselves, then if you *both* like antique furniture you can have half mine. They'd be coming to you anyway. And as much as Carys's Mum loved her things, I think even she would agree I don't need *two* Welsh dressers and *two* grandfather clocks.'

Carys got up and hugged me, which told me what *she* thought. 'Thanks, Dad,' she said 'You're the bestest Dad ever.'

Then she added.

'The same goes for you and Meryn. Take every moment of happiness while you can, both of you, like we're doing. You never know what's around the corner.'

You never know what's around the corner.

If only I'd known how prophetic those words were.

Looking back on it all now, I can see that much of what followed was influenced by what each of us involved understood by the meaning of that so emotive word *love*.

When it was over and I was able to cope again – though not too well – I looked it up in my Oxford Dictionary. And as I read its many definitions, I realised this was why so much of what went wrong, went wrong. Under the same one word is listed every type of affection under the sun. And so, when using the word verbally, there's no differentiating between "liking" and what *I've* always understood by "love".

And by that I mean… *real love.*

Finding the letter **L**, this is what I read:

> Love[1]: warm affection, liking or fondness, affectionate devotion (*of, for, towards* a person; *of, for*, or *to* a thing), paternal benevolence (esp. of God).

> Love[2]: **1.** hold dear, bear or make love to, be in love with, be fond of, love me, love my dog. **2.** be in love. **3.** cling to, delight in, enjoy having, be addicted to, admire or be glad of the existence of (life, honour, comfort, golf…).

Love of God bracketed with a *thing*, for goodness sake.

And one's love for a lover, and the love of one's child (and all their varying emotions: joy, ecstasy, pain) categorised with the love of an animal…and of a sport! Also, being *addicted* to something – drugs maybe. Hell's bells!

Forget the drugs, I've never been tempted. But take golf. I *like* golf. It's a great game. For four years I played to a handicap of 3, and in those heady days until I clicked my back trying to belt a ball too damned far with my driver, I liked it a lot. And though I don't play it anymore, it's still my favourite sport on tv – especially when Peter Allis was commentating. But to say I *love* it…come on, that's going a bit far.

As for dogs, okay, I admit I've never owned one. But when Ewen married my new and perfect daughter-in-law, Jessica, they bought a bearded collie with a name a mile long. They called him Harrison, "Harry" for short, it suited him. He was really winsome, endearing even, especially when he cocked his head to one side and looked at you with his big, brown, plaintive eyes. He was also nuts, totally and absolutely *bananas*, and gave us hours of laughter with the crazy, impossible things he tried to do. Like when he tried to jump that five-bar gate from a sitting position just because the urge to do so suddenly took him (mind you, if it wasn't for the fifth bar he'd have made it). But to say I *loved* him, even though a dog is said to be man's best friend – again, don't let's get carried away.

I love you.

These are the three precious words you whisper to your lover on waking up in the morning and seeing her oh-so-precious and familiar face sleeping next to yours on the pillow. Love is what causes the leap in your heart, and the joy in your soul, looking at her lying there, and then leaning over and kissing her on her forehead, or her cheek, or her lips…but tenderly, ever so tenderly, so as not to disturb her.

Love is the overwhelming emotion you feel when holding your own child in your arms. Especially the very first time you hold them. As they lie there, staring fixed and wide-eyed up at you, so trusting, and you smell that sweet smell new born babies have at the back of their necks, love is what causes you to swear, by all that's dear to you, that no harm will ever come to them…not if you can ever help it.

So, how can one's **LOVE** for a lover…

Or the **LOVE** for one's child…

Possibly be compared to the love of a pet, or a sport?

The answer, of course, is…They can't.

But there again, how can the **LOVE** you feel for your lover, be the *same* as the **LOVE** you feel for your precious daughter?

The answer again is it's not. It can't be. They're completely different emotions. Yes, I admit that both are overpowering, that both are like no love you've ever felt before, and that both can often, only too often, tear you apart.

But they're different. Absolutely…and totally…*different.*

And that's where the trouble started, you see.

Still looking back, I blame it on the first authors of the English language for using the same word "love" for every emotion of the heart, be it just liking…or the greatest of loves.

Especially when it comes to people.

And especially so for all of us who were part of everything that followed.

We make some attempt in Welsh.

Caru for the "love" of a person. *Hoffi* for the "liking" of a sport. It's not perfect, but it helps.

But if only those early English fathers had gone a step further than us and used the distinctions of the original Greek and Latin – *eros* for love between lovers, *paternus* for a father's love for a child, *fileo* for a child's love for a father –

then maybe much of what happened to us all need not to have done so.

In our relationships, I mean, not events. Sadly, we rarely have the power to shape events, especially me.

With me that seems to be Fate's prerogative.

But it's too late now.

And there's no going back.

- seven -

Meanwhile, with Carys's words, "Take every moment of happiness while you can," still in my ears, the very next day I "dragged" Meryn to a travel bureau, and ten days later we were on an Alitalia flight bound for magical Italy. It's a country I love. I'd live there, given half a chance, I can still remember myself thinking, and at the same time imagining it: a villa in the red Tuscan hills around Fiesole, overlooking the beautiful valley of the River Arno, to the distant ochre-red domes and rooftops of Florence.

Provided Meryn was with me that was. Who knew? Dreams can sometimes come true. Maybe if my second book did well…

As the plane climbed out of Manchester Airport and broke through the white clouds looking like a cotton wool carpet beneath us, into the sunshine and the clear blue sky above, Meryn put her arm through mine and clutched me tight. She'd been to other countries and faraway places, but this was her first time to Italy, and I couldn't wait to show it to her.

'This is just like a dream,' she said, her nearness combining with the smell of her perfume, giving me goose pimples tingling up and down my spine. 'It was all so sudden, I love surprises. A fortnight alone together, we're going to have a lovely time, I just know we are.'

'Almost like a honeymoon,' I said.

'I can't seem to remember you asking me to marry you,' she replied. 'Not properly. Not on one knee. But when you do, remember to make it special, or I could say no.'

It will be, I said to myself, thinking of the ring lying in a blue box lined with blue velvet inside my travel-bag (it was the right size, I'd checked one of her dress rings). What's more, I'd carefully chosen the hotel, and if it was anything like it claimed to be I had it all planned. In the photographs it looked perfect, romance itself set in lush gardens on the edge of cliffs, overlooking the blue sweep of the Bay of Naples and across to the Isle of Capri; and behind it, Sorrento, of ballad fame – back-dropped by heat-hazed wooded mountains, dominated by Mount Vesuvius.

The stuff of dreams…

Being something of a romantic (*Roman Holiday* – with Gregory Peck, Rachel's pin-up, and Audrey Hepburn, mine – was another of my favourite films) I intended for us to spend the first two days just relaxing in and around the hotel's beautiful pool, surrounded by a terracotta patio with pink and yellow honeysuckle spreading up its protective walls, and in the afternoon heat pull our sunbeds under the warm shade of leafy palm trees. Then in between taking it easy (I had it all worked out in my mind) we'd take a boat, or maybe drive, to see other romantic places: Positano with its gaily coloured villas clinging in tiers to a rock-ribbed hill-side falling away into the sea. The emerald isle of Ischia. Rome, the Eternal City, where we would throw coins into the Trevi Fountain and make our secret wishes. And Capri, where, after wandering the island, we'd find a secluded cove with a rocky pool of crystal clear blue water, and mine would be answered as we lazed in the sun and I would ask Meryn to marry me and she would say "yes". "Special" was what she wanted and "special" was what I had destined – a romantic proposal in a romantic setting, the ring would be a perfect fit, and that night we would become lovers and lie in each other's arms gazing out at a night-blue sky, cloudless and star speckled.

As I said, the stuff of dreams.

Both the two-days-around-the-pool bit and Positano went according to plan.

It was in Ischia that things started wandering away from the script.

We sailed into Porto Ischia on a blazing hot day, and all we could think of was Cokes in tall glasses filled with ice cubes. But the cafes were crowded, so we popped into the cool of a shop next to one and pretended to be looking at the wares, but keeping our eyes open for a shaded table to go empty. One fell vacant, I dashed to it, secured it, realised I'd left my floppy sun hat in the shop – it was a new one I'd bought especially back home – went back for it, saw I'd put it down on a shelf of similar hats for sale, picked it up and hurried out to rejoin Meryn.

Behind me, I heard a shout, but ignored it.

The next I knew was the shop-owner, an ample bosomed *signora* of a somewhat excitable temperament, snatching my hat from me and accosting me on the street, where, to a growing crowd of inquisitive onlookers – and Meryn, sitting at the table, doubled up with laughter and tears streaming down her face, *pretending not to know me* – the very irate lady accused me, in rapid Italian with accompanying hand and arm action, of stealing my own hat, and at the same time screaming volubly for the *polizia*.

Fortunately the police didn't arrive and it was eventually sorted out by my playing dumb – replying in Welsh and in sign-language, pointing to the label inside the hat and then to myself (*it's mine*) – until she reluctantly withdrew, still gesticulating and giving me dark looks over her shoulder, while muttering what seemed to be curses, as if wishing all manner of dire evils to descend on my head.

It was difficult being all cosmopolitan the rest of the day after that.

Two days later we drove to Rome. After showing Meryn the Coliseum, the Spanish Steps, St Peter's Basilica and so on, I was determined to redeem my image around the Trevi Fountain, something out of *Three Coins in the Fountain* was the sort of thing I had in mind, to make my wishes (and hopefully, Meryn's) come true.

The Trevi was closed for stone-blasting and repairs.

Ah, well, I consoled myself, there's still Capri...

As it happened, I'd not been to Capri before, and didn't know the island was tiered like a wedding cake, its ringed coastal area and the port itself, Marina Grande, constituting the bottom tier; Anacapri the top; and Capri the piece in the middle. So there was no rocky pool of crystal clear, azure water to swim in, no secluded cove to lie out in the sun, for me to pop the question.

So instead, I took Meryn to a scenic viewpoint on the summit of a high cliff, with the blue Mediterranean stretched far below us, dotted with white yachts, a most romantic setting for a proposal, took the box out of my pocket, opened it and showed Meryn the ring lying inside on blue velvet, took it out to place on her left third finger…and let it slip from my grasp to drop slowly, as if in slow motion, spiralling, ever decreasing in size, until it became too small to follow, on to the rocks far below.

I can still recollect the feeling of horror, and seeing Meryn looking down after it, this time not knowing whether to laugh, or to cry.

She did both, sort of half smiling with her eyes all moist. Then…

'Ah well, it looked a lovely ring, the little I saw of it,' she said, transferring a dress ring from her right hand to her left. 'And it was certainly special. Not *quite* what I had in mind, but the answer's still yes.'

That night, as we drifted to sleep in each other's arms, Meryn whispered to me in Welsh: *R'wyf fi'n dy garu di dros ben. Weld ti yn y bore.* (literal translation: "I love you over my head. See you in the morning.")

Next morning, I awoke to see her sleeping face next to mine on her pillow. Not wanting to disturb her, I looked at her silently, drinking her in.

'And now you're mine,' I thought, 'and I'm yours. Nothing will ever separate us, *nothing*, I'll make sure of that.'

Meryn opened her eyes. Looked at me for a long moment. And said: 'Have I told you how much I love you, Mr Rees.'

'And I love you, Miss Asher,' I replied.

She put her arm around my neck.

'We waited too long,' she said.

Later, much later, I said: 'I hope you don't have an Aunty Gwenda who'll turn up on our honeymoon.'

'No way,' Meryn replied. 'It's just you and me – secret destination and a "do not disturb" sign on the door.'

Aunty Gwenda?

No, I've not mentioned her before – but seeing as I've clearly told Meryn a true story about her, maybe now is as good a time as any to relate it.

Of how Aunty Gwenda was Rachel's closest aunt – and a most possessive one at that. Only a year old when her mother, *Nain* Bellis, died, only thirty-two, of ovarian cancer, she was brought up by a doting aunt, idolised by her oldest brother John – Rachel's father – and as a consequence, ruined to the point of her every wish (and whim) being always given in to.

She married a sheep farmer in Mid-Wales, who owned a ten-mile stretch of valley land and the hills on both sides. So, after he was killed when his horse threw him, bringing his flocks down to their winter grazing, Aunt Gwenda was left quite comfortably off.

She was also childless and as a consequence, when Rachel's father died – Rachel was only twelve at the time – Aunty Gwenda decided to take his place in her life, representative of the Bellis side of the family. Not only that, but with Rachel also happening to be her favourite niece, it meant we saw more of Aunt Gwenda than I, personally, would have wished.

Including on our honeymoon.

True.

Because when Rachel and I (one week back from Malaya and discharged from the army) arrived all lustful, at our London hotel – we'd chosen to drive down after saying goodbye to everyone at our wedding reception, but been held up on the way by heavy traffic – there, waiting to greet us in the foyer, was *Aunt Gwenda.*

'Where've you been?' she questioned, 'I was beginning to wonder if you were ever going to get here.' she prattled on, indifferent to my glares as she related how she'd guessed we'd choose a Forte hotel, and had rung their central office a few days earlier, and been told where we'd registered into…

I should have sued them.

…and after joining in all the "goodbye"-waving as we sped off, Aunt Gwenda had taken a taxi to Chester Station, then an Inter-City train to Euston, and finally a taxi again, reaching our hotel an hour before us, and was already firmly installed in her room – *next to us!*

'I've been on pins thinking you wouldn't make it in time,' she admonished, waving three tickets at us. 'I'm treating you to the theatre.'

Not wanting to offend her, Rachel tightened her lip and said nothing. Two hours later, on the *first night* of our honeymoon, the three of us were sitting together in the stalls, watching *Dial M for Murder* (an apt title considering the way I was feeling). The only consolation was that it was better than watching, *No Sex Please, We're British*. That *would* have been rubbing salt into the wound.

After the theatre, she took us out to dinner ('How thoughtful of you, Aunty Gwenda.' *Do I kill you now, or later?*) and we didn't get back to the hotel until gone two in the morning – for coffee in the lounge. ('Yes we'd *love* a coffee, Aunty Gwenda, really we would.' *Why don't we have it in the roof-garden lounge? I'll find you a rickety chair next to an open window, and make a wish as I've never made a wish before.*)

We (that's just Rachel and I) finally crawled into bed at gone three and fell straight to sleep.

Four hours later – at seven! – we were woken by Aunty Gwenda pounding on our door and calling out: 'Come on you two. Breakfast!', and expecting to be let into our room – which she wasn't. I drew the line at Aunt Gwenda watching me shower and get dressed.

She remained with us the whole week and travelled back with us in the car, to stay another week with us in our new home.

I'd told Meryn all this.

She thought it hilarious and had subjected me to much teasing about it.

'No, I've no Aunty Gwenda,' she reiterated. 'But I can ask Aunty Dilys to come with us, if you'd like?'

'No thanks,' I said.

- eight -

I know I've already touched on this earlier, Abigail, but as I was falling asleep last night, I again realised that when you reach the age for me (or Uncle Ewen) to give you this letter to read, you'll likely still be asking why am I telling you so much of what happened in the past.

Well, before we get to other things yet to come, I want you to know how much of a happy and normal family we once were, close despite our traits (Aunt Gwenda was very much a one-off, what we call "a character", and every family's entitled to one!). So, yes, normal and united, and looking forward to many happy years together.

And although I doubt you'll remember this, you were always asking me why I lived alone. Daddy had Mummy Ileana. Grandad Tony had Grandma Anne. Bunicu had Bunica. And Uncle Ewen had Aunty Jessy. Why didn't I have anyone? Well, I've now touched a little on this, the rest will follow…except to say it's all to do with how each of us reacts to adversity.

The way it either pulls us together.

Or drives us apart.

It's no one's fault, it's just the way it is.

I've told you that *Sleepless in Seattle* is one of my favourite films. I still watch it, and in the opening scene – the funeral of Tom Hanks' wife – his character, Sam, tries to somehow explain her death – much better than I'm able to – to his 8-year old son, Jonah.

Sam and Jonah are standing silent together by the side of her grave on a small hillside, silhouetted in dark suits against the sky. The other mourners have drawn to one side, leaving the two of them alone with their grief. Sam has his hand on Jonah's shoulder. From their body language it's clear Sam is very close to his son, and Jonah is comfortable with his Dad. They're supporting each other as they remember the person they've just buried. Sam – his wife. Jonah – his mum. But Sam feels he should try to explain her loss to Jonah, except he can't. He can't even explain it to himself, yet he does the best he can.

Mummy got sick (Sam says)
It happened just like that.
Nothing anybody could do.
It isn't fair.
No reason.
But if we asked the reason "why?"
We'd go crazy.

And that's exactly how I felt when Mummy Carys got sick.
It wasn't fair.
I couldn't see any reason behind it.
And asking "why?" just drove me crazy.
So, I found that the only thing to do.
The only thing to numb the mind.
The only thing to dull the pain.
Was to see each day through.

One at a time.
One at a time.
One at a time.

- nine -

'Meryn! Look at this! Isn't it *gorgeous*?'

We both turned to see Carys with her face pretty well pressed up against a glass showcase. She'd been so impatient for us to get back from Sorrento to help her look for a wedding dress, that less than ten hours after landing late on a Friday evening in Manchester and driving home to Trewrthymor, then getting up early next morning and driving almost the same journey back to Chester – we still had five minutes to wait for the first bridal shop to open before being let in.

Arriving back home, we (that's Meryn and I, but still minus a ring) had intended telling everyone our news. But when Carys told us she and Ian had set their wedding date for only six months away, we decided to keep it our secret – we wanted the time to be theirs, and just theirs. And I still had the old house to sell. Meryn was still adamant she didn't want to live in it, and I understood her reluctance. I'd have felt the same if it was the other way around.

But I never realised how much there was to be done in organising a wedding. With typical efficiency, Carys had opened a folder for it and compiled a list. Though only in first draft it was *already* a mile long. Arranging the church, cars, quotes for the reception, choosing the cake (I'd *no idea* there could be such a fuss over a cake).

As for the bridesmaids, they were already decided. Donna, Ian's younger sister, and Emma, Carys's cousin (my brother Matthew's daughter). Both nineteen, the same height as Carys, both with urchin-cuts, and as brown as berries from recent holidays abroad.

And Sara, my precious Sara, Ewen and Jessy's daughter, my first grandchild, was to be the flower-girl. I thought the world of her. Two years old and gorgeous with it, she was already showing signs of being a dreamy individual. Not that that was a defect, Carys was also dreamy when she was young, with adolescent crushes (pre a later Mr Darcy period) on Donny and Cliff. In fact – and despite their age-gap – she was going to marry Cliff when she was five, but then he two-timed her by going out with Sue Barker and she never forgave him.

Ah well, Cliff's loss, Ian's gain.

I also had a grandson, Nathan – Sara's brother – and I loved him very much too. Six months old, he was really cute and destined to grow up tall and handsome, I could tell, he looked just like photos of me when I was that age. Rachel would have idolised them both, she'd have been the original, doting "Gammy". Baby sit? Ewen and Jessy could have gone out every night.

But I'm digressing again…

We turned to look at the wedding dress. It was a delicate shade of pink, just a whisper of it under white lace. Fit for a princess.

'It's beautiful, Carys,' Meryn said. Carys asked to try it on and, being female, of course took two more – one: white, the other: ivory – with her into the changing room.

She emerged first in the lacy shell pink.

Not only was it fit for a princess, she looked just like a princess in it.

I said, 'It's perfect, Carys. No need to bother with the other two.'

'Dad!' Carys protested: 'I *have* to try them on as well.'

'Why?' I asked. 'You won't find anything prettier, not if we're here until Doomsday.'

This time Meryn objected. 'Oh, Luke! Have a heart. Carys can't *possibly* decide on the first dress she puts on.' She turned to this very fussy daughter of mine and they both raised their eyebrows, as if to say: 'He's a *man*, what else can you expect?'

But naturally, I was justified, because the other two weren't a patch on the first.

Carys tried it on again. It was as if it had been made for her.

'It's perfect, Carys,' I said again. 'Made for you. What do you think, Meryn?'

'It's absolutely beautiful, Carys,' Meryn said. 'You wouldn't have found anything nicer if we'd gone up to London to look. It doesn't even need altering. Fits you like a glove. It's as if it was waiting there just for you.'

Great! We were agreed. I turned to the sales-lady, 'We'll take it,' only to be met by two howls of protest naming other bridal-shops we'd not yet visited.

Very reluctantly, as if bestowing a royal favour, the sales-lady agreed to put the dress on hold for an hour, but no more. A second over and it would be back in the showcase.

Fifty-nine minutes later, after a whistle-stop dash around every other bridal shop in the city (or so it seemed, we couldn't possibly have missed one out) I'd been sent ahead by both Carys and Meryn to reach the first shop in time, with the added threat from my usually gentle daughter of goodness-knows-what if I failed.

Another thirty seconds and I was charging in through their front doors, missing out the lift and tearing up the stairs, reaching the Bridal Department looking like that old film clip of the English long-distance runner – Jim something-or-other...Jim Peters, that was it – finishing a Commonwealth Games marathon, legs wobbling like jelly, not knowing if he was in Vancouver or Timbuktu (it was Vancouver) just as the dress emerged from the changing room on its way back to the showcase.

By the time Carys and Meryn arrived, it was already paid for and boxed, and I was ready for home. I'd not realised we'd only just started.

There were still piles of head-dresses to try on, and seemingly hundreds of shoes, matching material to buy for the bridesmaids' dresses and...oh, heaven-only-knows what else.

But finally, four hours later we were finished (for me in more ways than one; I was finished physically and mentally – and financially, with the wedding reception still to pay for) and on our way home, Carys sitting in the back, happily smothered under her mountain of purchases.

'Oh,' she exclaimed through them all, the excitement of it still in her voice. 'It's been a lovely, fantastic day.'

Looking back now, I'm so glad she enjoyed it.

So very, very, glad.

As we neared home, Meryn turned to my precious daughter: 'Is Aunty Gwenda going with you on honeymoon, Carys?'

'No way!' my daughter exclaimed. 'Not if she disinherits me.'

The wedding was perfect.

Though it was mid-October, the weather was glorious, not a cloud in sight, and it all went off without a hitch. Everything planned to the nth degree. But that was Carys...

Apart from keeping her bedroom tidy.

But I was going to miss terribly all that confusion of clothes strewn all over the place – bed, chairs, floor, everywhere except in the wardrobes and chests where they belonged.

Both bridesmaids looked beautiful, alike as two peas in a pod, their almost russet shade dresses subtly toning in with Carys's shimmering-pink-under-white-lace dress.

And my precious Sara, bless her, following them down the aisle in the same russet colour, looking so pretty and adorable carrying her wicker flower basket, not putting a foot wrong. And as for the bride and groom, Ian was handsome in his morning suit, Carys radiant.

And to top it all, Ewen gave his "little" sister a big hug.

What's more *in public,* right outside the church when she arrived, to tell her "you look fantastic, sis", and wish her "every happiness".

That really sealed the day for her...except...

Looking back on it now from a distance, I think it was fortunate we don't have the power to see what's ahead of us, or it would have ruined the day for us. But the only thing that mattered then was that it all went smoothly.

And it did.

In my father-of-the-bride speech at the reception in *Plas-ar-Hendir* (where, in effect, it all started, when Meryn said to me, 'If it's to be, it's to be.') just close friends and immediate family, I restricted myself to giving my new son-in-law but one piece of good advice – drawing on my own personal experience, so succinctly put by the American poet, Ogden Nash:

If you wish to keep love brimming
in your marriage cup.
Whenever you're wrong, admit it.
Whenever you're right, shut up.

A wedding's a great place to make a speech. No matter how badly a funny quote is told, everyone feels obliged to laugh, if only dutifully – even Aunt Gwenda, even she laughed – on the day, at least. But when she died a year later of a heart attack, we discovered that the first thing she did on getting back home from the wedding, was to go straight to her solicitors and cut me out as the main beneficiary of her Will – leaving me an antique writing bureau instead.

Her reason? Well, after Rachel died, Aunt Gwenda made it more than clear to me that my example for the rest of my life should be her own father, Jonathan – who mourned his wife, Elisabeth, for twenty years after she died from ovarian cancer, before dying himself of a broken heart. At the reception I'd introduced Meryn to her. And to Aunt Gwenda, Meryn was a betrayal of my love for Rachel.

The bureau was a beautiful piece of furniture – on the outside. Inside, it was all woodworm and had to be burnt.

I wonder if Aunt Gwenda knew?

Ah, well, if it made her happy.

As the taxi grew smaller, with Carys waving furiously out of the window – they were bound for a fortnight "somewhere in the sun" (Algarve, I'd overheard them discussing it) – I looked down at the parting gift she'd pressed into my hand.

It was a green leather book-marker, with words inscribed in gold that made me bite my lip to hold back my tears. Strong in her faith, Carys would have meant its maxim, not chosen it lightly.

The greatest gift
I ever had
came from God
I call him DAD

I put my arm around Meryn's waist and pulled her close, defying a gimlet look from Aunt Gwenda. 'I'm so glad I listened to you, the day I first met Ian,' I said, 'And thanks for agreeing to put us on hold. I'll make it up to you,' I vowed, and meaning it. 'I've dropped the house-price another ten percent, life's too short waiting for this crazy recession to lift. That should be enough to swing it, but if not I'll drop it some more. I'm not letting a pile of bricks and mortar stop us from being together.'

It was a simple promise.

If only life itself was so simple.

And its purposes easy to understand.

- ten -

The next morning I awoke early.

I always sleep with my curtains open.

The blue skies of yesterday had been replaced by dark clouds coming in heavy and low over the mountains.

Soon they were overhead, bringing with them wisps of mist, followed by a curtain of rain, changing the blue waters of the bay into grey, whipping up angry waves crested in white.

And obscuring the view.

- eleven -

I still don't close my curtains, Abigail, and last night as I fell asleep I thought I heard a voice whisper in the darkness: "See you in the morning."

It couldn't have been my imagination, my background doesn't allow it.

Soldiers on patrol have no time to wonder, their reactions have to be instinctive.

Accountants are without imagination – except for creative bookkeeping.

Writers put all their imaginings into stories, leaving none left for themselves.

It was a female voice. Whispered in English that narrowed it down to four.

When I was a child and my mam tucked me up in bed before blowing out the candle – our only nightlight then, living out in the wilds electricity hadn't yet reached us, nor had plumbing other than one cold water tap – bath time for Matthew and me was in a kettle-filled tin tub by the fire, and our privy was at the bottom of the garden, far from the house and bitterly cold to go out to in the winter – she said those words to me in Welsh, which ruled my mother out.

And so, my resultant dream was a jumble of your Gammy Rachel, and Mummy Carys, and Meryn.

And you, of course.

"See you in the morning," were the last words Rachel whispered to me every night for four months before we fell asleep, ever since we were told that's how long she had to live. Not that I slept much, only cat-napped on the sofa alongside her bed, holding her hand. She meant by them more than just "see you tomorrow" – much, much more. If, when I opened my eyes, I was to find she wasn't already awake and regarding me with that steady look of hers, she meant in Eternity.

Carys also whispered the same words to me as her life ebbed away in hospital; she lying in bed in her softly lit room and me in a put-you-up chair holding her hand – just as I did with Rachel. The last time she said them was on Ian's evening to be alone with her, and as I kissed her "goodnight, precious sweet heart" and held her frail body in my arms, she whispered them to me in such a way we both knew it was for the last time here on Earth and, like Rachel, she meant them as her promise that the next time we'd see each other would be in Heaven.

Except where is Heaven?

Somewhere out there, we were told as children, and as children we believed it, somewhere out there in deep space, way, way above the dark blue vastness, and far beyond the panoply of stars.

But now I ask myself, is it only in our hearts, a panacea for our grief? I once thought I knew, I don't any more, yet I like to think that Rachel and Carys are out there somewhere, and with that thought, I look up and imagine they can see me, and I smile up at them and wink, "I won't be too long…"

Meryn also used to utter the same promise. As well as saying it in English, she'd sometimes murmur it in Welsh. But now I find myself wondering did she really mean it when she said it, not just for one tomorrow, but for a lifetime of them, and that only the cruelty of life prevented it from happening?

But I guess I'll never know.

As for you sixpence…well, you preferred me to say "see you later alligator", for you to giggle back "in a while cwocodile", and wait all expectant for me to come snap-snapping back at you, play acting like I wanted to eat you, and you would hide crouched up under the duvet and I'd pretend not to notice the giggling lump you made, and frantically search for you, crying: 'Oh, Abigail's gone. Where is she? What am I going to do?'

At which you'd surface with a *woosh*, shouting,'I'm here, Gaga, I'm here.'

And wrap your chubby arms around my neck and kiss away my sham tears.

I'm so glad I was able to make those times happy for you, sweetheart; as for me they were precious, an oasis of joy in a desert of pain…

Of course, hearing the words in the darkness may have been my wishful thinking.

I was feeling tired, a little bit low, and so, not wanting to brood, I tried pushing you all out of my mind, but none of you would go away.

Lying there in the darkness, I could hear the whisper being repeated: "See you in the morning. See you in the morning…"

But I still couldn't decide which of you was whispering them.

And that's how I fell asleep, still hearing them.

But once again I'm digressing, so getting back to the morning after Mummy and Daddy left on honeymoon and the black clouds coming in over the mountains; by lunchtime they'd gone, the sky was back to blue, and the waters of the bay were still again. Deciding it was the Celt in me seeing portends where none existed, I dismissed them from my mind and drove to Meryn's and took her out for lunch, then we started house hunting.

In the twelve months that followed my foreboding everything went great for us all. Also, I'd completed my first draft of *The Reikel Conspiracy* (the *Mary Celeste* story) and during a necessary break from it before getting down to final editing and polishing it, had started a third, *Twice Upon a Thanksgiving*, two parallel love stories set in the "New World", one in today's time, the other four hundred years back to when the Pilgrim Fathers first set foot there.

Unfortunately, the property market hadn't improved, and the house still wasn't sold, but Meryn had finally agreed to live in it after we were married – in three months' time, with our honeymoon destination chosen: Italy, where else? After Sorrento, she loved it as much as I did and this time we'd chosen Santa Margherita on the beautiful Ligurian coast, east of Genoa.

What's more, to crown it all…and to put icing on the cake.

(Using a mixed metaphor here, Abigail – Daddy will tell you what it means)

You were on the way.

- twelve -

I was opening a parcel of research books just arrived by post from The London Library, when the phone rang.

It was Carys, she sounded frightened.

'Daddy, can you come right over, I'm in pain. I'm frightened I'm losing my baby.'

She was five months pregnant and had been ill almost from the start. I was usually with her from first thing in the morning, getting there before Ian left at 7.30 for his work, taking my note pads and research books for the day with me. But today I'd had to wait for the books to arrive, and rang her earlier, told her I'd be delayed.

'That's okay,' she'd said, 'I'm feeling better today. Do what you have to and don't worry, I'll be all right…' but then she'd paused and added, 'Love you, Daddy.'

I should have taken more notice of that pause and detected the catch in her voice when she said 'Love you, Daddy,' and realised she was putting on a brave face, trying to reassure me that everything was fine with her.

In less than a minute I was in my car, tearing down the road.

They lived two miles away. Today, I knew Ian was working in a part of the forest twenty miles up into the mountains, along narrow, twisting Welsh roads, which at this time of the year were even more testing to drive, with tourist coaches negotiating S-bends in low gears, making it impossible to pass them. In summer, the journey could take over an hour. Knowing he would take risks to be with her, this was why Carys had phoned me back.

But as Ian prized doing everything for her, if it looked serious, ringing him would be top of my list.

I took risks myself and despite 30 mph signs and traffic lights on red, screeched to a halt outside their house – a split-level on a hillside – in just over five minutes, then ran up their zig-zagging sidepath and in through the back door.

Everywhere was silent.

'Carys!' I called out, all apprehensive.

'In here, Dad,' her stifled voice came from the bedroom.

I hurried through to her.

She was lying on the bed, her face white and clammy, holding her stomach and doubled up in agony. She stretched out an arm to me, wanting to be held.

I did so, tried to reassure her that everything would be fine and broke away. Ian had gone to second on my list.

'Have you phoned Jane?' – Carys's young GP, they were on first name terms.

'No, I didn't want to trouble her.' Carys was almost crying…with pain, or from fear…or maybe both. 'I thought at first it might be gripe.'

'But it isn't?'

'No," she grimaced. 'It's getting worse. Daddy, I think I'm losing my baby.

'No way, Cara, it's something you've eaten.' To myself, I wasn't so sure, she looked really ill. 'But I'll call her,' I said, reaching for the phone and forcing myself to sound calm. 'Just to be on the safe side.'

Jane was also my GP and I knew her number. She said she'd be right over and so I released Carys's hand, telling her I was going to make her a hot cup of tea to see if it would help ease the pain. But this was for me to phone Ian from the kitchen to his mobile, asking him not to take risks getting home, because I was here and Jane was on her way.

Ian made it in less than thirty minutes.

I didn't ask "how?". Knowing those bends, lined by dry stone walls, and the river raging below it, whatever the time of year, I preferred *not* to know, other than putting it down to the stock car driver in him. He tore up the stairs two at a time and straight into the bedroom. From the sitting-room, I heard Carys cry out with relief to see him.

And I too was glad because Jane had just finished examining her and was with me, phoning for an ambulance.

Oh, Carys.

The ambulance arrived soon after, I didn't wait to see it go around the corner, ran back into the house, made hurried phone calls to let everyone know what was happening, got into my car and tore down the motorway after it.

And before I knew it, the hospital came into sight.

Carys was lying in a ward bed, still in agony, waiting for a doctor. Ian was sitting beside her, holding her hand. On her stomach to help alleviate the pain, was a warm-pack. Remembering my own experience some years back, when I applied a hot water bottle to what I thought was stomach-ache, and almost perforated my appendix, I removed it.

'Luke?' Ian objected. 'Shouldn't you leave it? They know what they're doing.'

I explained my concern, adding that my paternal granddad had died from peritonitis and my father almost did, it could be a family inherited thing. But I could see I'd not persuaded him and he was about to replace the warm-pack, when a nurse crossed to the bed and did it for him.

'What if it's an appendix?' I asked, voicing my fear.

'That's for *Mr* Rankin to decide,' she stated. 'He's been called and shouldn't be too long.'

Hearing her stress the *"Mr"*, I realised she was referring to a consultant, but I didn't much care for her, "*shouldn't* be *too* long*". I would have preferred a more positive statement like "I can see him running". If it *was* an appendix and it burst because of the warm-pack before he got to Carys, she could likely lose her baby, and possibly her own life.

And *I* would never forgive myself for not arguing back.

'I'm sorry,' I persisted, 'but while we're waiting for him, we could be risking peritonitis. With Carys having a baby, surely that could be fatal? To *both*,' I stressed. 'Shouldn't you–'

The nurse ended the discussion by turning away. I was still uneasy and again removed the pack. She was watching for me to do exactly that, placed it back and faced me.

Stand-off…

But before our sparring even began, a young man with a stethoscope entered the ward in a hurry and straight to Carys's bed. I assumed him to be Mr Rankin and retreated.

Moments later, Ian joined me in the waiting room. Neither of us mentioned the incident and we were pacing the floor hoping that whatever was causing Carys's pain it wasn't serious, when we saw two nurses with a trolley race past the open door, pursued by the stethoscoped young man.

Carys was on it, covered by a sheet and an oxygen mask clamped over her face.

Ian and I both made for the door. The nurse entered. Ian tried to push past her, demanding to know what was happening. She asked us to sit down and waited until we reluctantly did.

'Mr Rankin thinks it's an appendix,' she told us, in not quite her assertive voice of before. 'Carys is on her way to theatre for an op.'

'An appendix!' Ian protested. 'But Cris is having a baby!'

'Mr Rankin's a top surgeon. For him it's a routine procedure.'

'But she's five months pregnant,' Ian persisted. I could hear the anguish in his voice.

'That should be no problem. We'll let you know if we hear something.'

That SHOULD be no problem.

What does *SHOULD* mean...

And what's meant by...*IF we hear something*...

'Would either of you like something while you're waiting? Tea? Coffee? Chocolate?'

Two lives were at risk and we were being offered something from a vending machine.

And not only that, but *choices*. At a time like this.

77

'But how much risk is there?' Ian begged, ignoring the offer.

'Carys couldn't be in better hands. Are you sure I can't get you anything…'

We dumbly shook our heads and she left the room.

Ian buried his face in his hands. At that moment, Anne and Tony hurried past the open door and saw us. Entering the room, they went straight to Ian to comfort him.

I crossed to the window. Standing there, I felt no satisfaction in having my fear proved right.

An appendix. A bloody appendix.

I would have given anything to be wrong, for it to be nothing more than a stomach disorder.

Instead, my precious daughter's life was in danger.

As was the baby's she so much wanted.

Looking through the window at the flat empty fields stretching before me, I could glimpse the sea in the distance.

Today it looked grey.

- thirteen -

I was sitting in my car on a lonely stretch of the beach.

Realising there was nothing I could do at the hospital – not with Ian having his Mum and Dad there – and rather than sit on my own going crazy with worry waiting to hear whether Carys and her baby were going to be okay, I'd driven here to be alone with my thoughts.

Why couldn't Carys's pregnancy have been normal? Like ninety-nine percent of women who carry without problems? And *why* Carys? She'd been so looking forward to holding her new born baby in her arms.

Why, why, why, I questioned as my mind went back to when I was holding her in *my* arms, only a minute old, seeing her open her eyes and giving me *that* smile, the one that had bonded my heart to hers for as long as I lived.

And in Heaven too, if there *is* such a place and I'm allowed in when I part my mortal coil.

To ask God what was he playing at?

I'm not trying to get profound here, nevertheless I don't think it's an unnatural thing to do. It's part of our human frailty, it seems to me, to turn, if only superstitiously, to some Higher Power for help – for answers – in moments of crisis. Even among those who claim not to have any kind of faith, many still find themselves doing it – though most will deny it after.

So, there I was, alone in my car on a deserted beach, less than a mile from where, at that same moment, my beautiful daughter was being operated on, looking up at the heavens and wondering, as I'd so often done in my life, was there *really* a God up there?

As I pondered, I could see the waves curling and breaking on the shore. Their tidal pattern, governed by the moon's gravitational pull, reminded me of the order of things on this, our earthly planet – and in the universe, of which we are but an infinitesimal part.

It spoke to me of a God. But what sort of God?

The *Abba* "Daddy" God I was brought up to pray to – the New Testament God that is, He's not so caring in the Old – told by my chapel-going mother that *"Duw cariad yw"*, "God is love".

Or some Supreme Being who formed the cosmos for some peculiar whim of his own, and left it at that, for things to take a random evolutionary course?

For years, as I'd watched the nightly TV news and seen the cruelty and barbarity, especially when it came to children, taking place right across our globe – and often in the very *name* of religion – doubts had crept more and more into my mind.

What about *suffer little children to come unto me*? I thought, my mind going back to when I drove overnight to South Wales after hearing the news of the terrible Aberfan pit disaster, to help dig away the slurry when a waste-tip slid down the mountain, engulfing the village school. Of the 144 that died that day, 116 were children, but despite the odds being against it, we dug for days in the hope of finding just one still alive.

We didn't, but despite it being a man-created tragedy, wouldn't a loving *Abba* God who knows all things have intervened, and made it happen an hour earlier at eight in the morning, *before* these little ones were in school, instead of waiting for them to be seated at their desks, maybe saying their morning prayers? If only He'd done that, those hundred and sixteen innocent children wouldn't have died. Died so needlessly.

Brooding on this, and other such catastrophes, when other innocent children had lost their lives…

In earthquakes. Floods. Tsunamis.

And at the hands of mind-crazed men. So-called religious fanatics indiscriminately blowing up babies along with adults. Even claiming they do it at the express will of their particular deity.

It didn't make any sense.

And so I closed my eyes, and instead forced my mind across the half-mile or so to where Carys was being operated on in theatre.

To be very honest, the nature of God – *if* He existed – was of little significance to me at that moment. What mattered was that my precious daughter's life lay in the hands of Mr Something-or-other Rankin. I didn't know his first name, but I prayed for them to be steady.

I glanced at my watch, saw I'd been there an hour, switched on my mobile and called Carys's ward, then asked to speak to Ian.

'Any news, Ian?'

'None, Luke, she's still in theatre.'

Hearing the stress still in his voice I thought of returning, but I couldn't bear the thought of being cooped up in a room so close to Carys yet be unable to do anything to help her. It was out of my hands…and I felt so impotent…so damned *impotent*.

'Are your Mum and Dad still with you?'

'Yes, they're still here.'

In that case – I decided – I'll walk the beach, and let the cold wind coming in from the Irish Sea numb me.

'I'll phone you back in a half an hour'

'Okay, Luke, God bless.'

'Ring you later,' I repeated, unable to respond to his exhortation. I first wanted proof that God cared – and that meant bringing Carys through.

'Ian? Any news?'

This time his voice was vibrant. 'Yes, it *was* an appendix, they caught it just in time, it was close to perforating. Cris is back from theatre, she's sleeping…' his voice choked, 'and both she and baby are fine.'

I let out a sigh of relief. *An appendix. Just an appendix. That's all it was in the end. Not what I'd secretly been fearing.* My eyes flooded with tears. My hands wouldn't stop trembling. I could hardly hold the phone.

'I'll be there in five minutes, Ian.'

There was silence as Ian recovered himself. Then, 'Would you make it tomorrow, Luke?' Mum and Dad have only just left, after peeping in on Cris; they've not eaten since breakfast. It was a bigger operation than they first thought, she's not to be disturbed. They've given her a room on her own, and made up a bed for me to be there for her when she wakes up.'

'Then I'll see you tomorrow, Ian. Give Carys my love when she comes round.'

'I will. God bless again.'

'God bless.' This time I could say it. 'And get yourself something to eat.'

Clearing the phone I opened the car window, feeling the cold wind on my face, and letting the tenseness of the last hours seep out of me.

Then I rang Ewen and Jessy. Both were thrilled.

And then I called Meryn. I wasn't seeing her this evening, Ian always worked late at his desk on Tuesdays, catching up with his admin, and I stayed with Carys until he got home.

'Hi, it's me -' I said. She cut across me.

'I've been sitting by the phone waiting for you to ring. Is Carys all right?'

'She is now. It was an appendix, but she was in theatre for—'

'Oh, what a relief. You can tell me about it when you get here. How long will you be?'

'Twenty minutes.'

'Have you eaten?'

'Not since breakfast.'

'Then I'll have something waiting. Don't be any later or it will go cold.'

'I won't, I'm starting off now.'

'Drive carefully. We've had enough upset for today.'

'I will,' I said. 'Love you.'

'I love you, too, Mr Rees,' Meryn said.

Click. She replaced her phone.

Tuesdays?

But of course – it had escaped me.

Ian wouldn't be working late *this* Tuesday.

He was spending the night in hospital with Carys.

And I could stay over with Meryn.

I needed to see her face on the pillow next to mine in the morning.

- fourteen -

We were chatting the next day around her hospital bed, Carys, Ian, and myself.

A big weight had been lifted from us knowing why she'd been feeling so ill, and we were laughing together and looking forward to Christmas–

When the door opened and Mr Rankin came in, clutching a file.

From his nervous smile and pained look in his eyes through rounded glasses, I instantly knew something was wrong.

So did Carys. The joy went from her face as he approached the bed.

Oh, no, what now!

Ian was sitting alongside Carys, his arm around her shoulders. Instinctively, he sensed the atmosphere and pulled her closer, holding her tight. I sat stock-still in my chair. Felt a dread fear rise within me again. Deep down in my soul I pleaded for it not to be right.

Carys was unable to remain silent. Whatever it was, she had to know.

'What is it? Is it my baby? Has the operation harmed it?'

'Baby's fine, Carys' Mr Rankin assured her, giving her a tender smile. Already, he was fond of this daughter of mine, I could tell by his gentleness with her. 'You have a real fighter there.'

He sat on the bed, removed his round rimmed glasses, and fidgeted with them. Though he had to cope daily with traumas, it was in this young man to be caring.

'This is always the most difficult part of my work.'

Carys gave a cry of anguish. I can hear it still, as if she had been stabbed in the heart with a knife, anticipating what Mr Rankin was going to tell her. Her eyes opened wide, like those of a frightened fawn's.

'I'm sorry, Carys…I wish there was an easy way to say this, but I'm afraid the appendix showed secondary cancer.'

Carys's face went pale. Ian tightened his arm around her. But other than that, neither gave any reaction, the blow had been too sudden.

As for me, having my worst fear confirmed, I went cold. Couldn't speak, couldn't move.

Mr Rankin replaced his glasses, adopted a normal tone. 'I'm waiting for the biopsy results, but I saw no trace of it elsewhere. So, with your previous op and family history, Carys – though we'll need a scan to confirm it – the most likely source is ovarian.'

Carys buried her face into Ian's chest and clung to him. But there were no tears, she was too stunned for tears.

I wanted to cross to the bed, to hold her, to stroke her head, and tell her everything would be alright, as I had done in the past.

Except, I couldn't. This was something beyond me, tearing me in two. What's more, my precious daughter now had Ian first in her life. And so I stayed where I was, feeling numb as I watched him try to soothe her. Seeing her shoulders shaking was tearing my very soul. Goodness knows what she must be thinking, what she must be feeling, she must be going through mental hell.

Oh, Carys, Cara, if only I could take it from you…

She raised her face. Her expression, as she looked at the young man with the dark blue corduroy trousers, blue striped shirt and stethoscope, was pleading, begging him to say she'd heard it wrong. That there was a possibility he might be mistaken. To make it even more heart breaking, her plea was so plain to see in her hazel eyes – yet she couldn't say the words.

Seeing her conflict, Mr Rankin flicked through his file as if studying his notes. I'm sure he didn't need to refer to any papers, the facts were stored in his mind; it was all for Carys's benefit, to give her strength, to dare her to hope.

He looked up and cleared his throat – until now I'd thought all surgeons had to be detached from what was happening around them.

'On a more positive note, Carys, your appendix can be regarded as a blessing in disguise, giving us early warning. Also – to repeat – there was no sign of cancer elsewhere, no adhesions to other organs. So, once the scan confirms it *is* ovarian, a hysterectomy should give you every hope of a full recovery–'

'A hysterectomy,' Carys protested. 'But that would mean losing my baby.'

There was deep regret in the young man's voice. 'I'm sorry, Carys…my advice is that we operate as soon as we get the results.'

'But what if we wait?' Carys begged him; begged him to the point of pleading again. 'And how long *can* we wait?'

He tried giving her a smile of encouragement, but it was more like pulling a wry face.

'Well…' Evincing his own upset by again removing his round glasses and polishing them with a white hanky, he pursed his lips as he worked it out. 'For *Baby* to have a fair chance – two months before we can think of inducing it. But for *your* sake, to prevent the cancer spreading, I wouldn't leave it any longer.'

Carys was suddenly alerted to another fear. 'But if it's ovarian, does that mean…that my baby…' She choked on her words.

The young man knew what Carys was asking and tried to answer her in as gentle a tone as he could. 'If that's the option you're thinking of taking, we won't know for Baby until after the birth. For you, Carys – as to whether we've caught it in time – I'm afraid not until after the op,'

He got to his feet. 'I'll leave you and Ian to talk it over. Should you decide against having the hysterectomy now, we'll be seeing each other regularly to monitor your progress. So, my name's Guy, less formal than Mr Rankin.' He moved to the door.

'Thank you, Mr…Guy,' Carys managed to reply, though her mind, every part of her being must have been churning. 'We'll do that…discuss it, then let you know. But for me, I already know I want to wait…

'*I want to have my baby.*'

- fifteen -

I want to have my baby.

With Carys's words still in my ears, I left her and Ian alone to talk and drove down to the same quiet stretch of beach as yesterday, to be alone with my thoughts again.

I knew she wouldn't change her mind. Not Carys. Not only had she always longed for a child, she would make a wonderful mother. The nursery at home was already waiting. Cot, baby clothes, shawls, teddy-bears, the lot. No, she wouldn't even *contemplate* a hysterectomy.

And so I'd come to the same spot again to be angry with God.

But instead, I was angry with–

Well, let me tell you why I was so uptight.

A year after Carys's previous operation to remove her benign cysts, our then incumbent government withdrew its funding for the screening programme she was on, and so saving themselves £1,000 per woman, per annum. At that time there were 200 women, all deemed "high-risk", on the same six-monthly, early warning scheme. If my calculation was right (I checked it again to make sure I'd not left out a nought) that was a *monumental* cut of £200,000 they made to their annual health budget.

£200,000…The price of five government Jags. And their deputy PM had *two* of them.

Was it *worth* it Mr Chancellor – Mr Prime Minister as he

afterwards became? Please tell me? Leaving the lives of 200 women at risk?

£200,000, having not long since sold 400 tonnes of gold bullion at a 20-year low in the market for only £2.3 billion, which if he'd kept it would today be worth £12-14 billion.

And Carys's funding needn't have been withdrawn.

Was it worth it, Mr B? Saving 200 grand? Tell me, please. Because I'd really like to know.

This isn't me trying to play politics for some Machiavellian reason. It really isn't. At that moment it seemed to me that whichever party was in power, Labour or Tories, the only man who ever went to Parliament with a good idea was Guy Fawkes.

And with that thought, I tried to get back to God.

But I couldn't get angry with Him, no matter how much I strove to.

After all, it wasn't God who decided the policies of governments.

Nevertheless, I just hoped He existed.

And that He was listening.

Because *if* He did.

And *if* He was.

And *if* the New Testament was true.

Then just as it's said He gave His only son for the sake of others.

Then please, I prayed…

Please let me give my life for my daughter.

Please take me.

Let me be your propitiation.

And let Carys live.

- sixteen -

As I drove to Meryn's, I was working it all out in my mind.

Two months before the baby could be induced.

And for Carys to recover from an appendectomy that was major.

Then another month until the hysterectomy could be performed.

That made it three months...

To when Meryn and I were getting married.

Except, I knew she wouldn't want to go ahead with it now, the anticipation would be taken out of it for her knowing Carys would be in hospital, unable to attend the wedding. Nor, like me, would Meryn dream of going away on honeymoon until we were told the operation was a success and the disease caught in time.

And if it was – I prayed with all my heart it would be – then with the baby being two months premature and needing feeding almost constantly through both day and night, and add to that the time it would take Carys to be sufficiently recovered from it all to be strong enough, and well enough, to again manage on her own...

All in all, it would be more like six months than three – and Ian's new employers couldn't be expected to give him that amount of time off.

If Rachel was alive she'd have cared for them, but she wasn't, and so it was up to me, as Carys's father, to now play my part.

But with all the delays Meryn and I had already experienced, I was going to be asking a lot of her to postpone it once more.

As I pulled up outside her house, I was hoping she'd understand.

I needn't have worried.

'Of course I understand,' she said, taking hold of both my hands. 'Carys comes first.'

She paused. 'I must admit I'm disappointed. I know it's only an extra three months, but at this moment it feels years away and I was so looking forward to being Mrs Rees.' She gripped my hands tight to reassure me it was okay. 'But we couldn't have gone ahead with it, not with this cloud hanging over us, so let's just look forward to Carys getting the all clear.'

She paused again. 'They *will* catch it in time, won't they? There's no chance of…Or the baby…'

She left both questions unfinished.

'Everything will fine,' I replied, trying to dampen my own fears. 'First the baby, then the operation. Six months from now it will all be over and we'll all be celebrating. And you and I will be back to walking up the aisle.'

'Oh, I hope so,' Meryn said.

She looked at me, her eyes glistening.

'I love you, Mr Rees,' she said.
'I love you, too, Miss Asher,' I said back.
One in a million, I thought, that was Meryn.

- seventeen -

To help me through the next three months, Abigail, I made myself think of the appendix in the same way as Guy Rankin – as a "blessing in disguise". An inherent malfunction from my side of the family, giving your Mummy warning of the inherent disorder on Gammy Rachel's side. That maybe some divine hand had brought Gammy and me together all those years ago to ensure that Mummy's disease would be caught in time.

I've already mentioned my appendix almost perforating – they operated on me just in time. My father wasn't quite so lucky; his did perforate, and for days it was touch and go whether he'd pull through. As for *his* father, my *Taid* (grandfather – pronounced "tide") living in those days of crushed stone roads and 15-mph ambulances, his appendix burst on the way to hospital and he died that same day. I never knew him, only from his photograph, but he looked just like David Ben Gurion, the first Prime Minister of Israel (maybe nullifying my belief I'm a full-blown Celt?) when, in 1948, the Jews were given back their homeland, after being dispersed from it by the Romans, almost 2,000 years before.

His wife, my *Nain* – *Nain* Frondeg as we called her, after the village she lived in – spent the rest of her forty-three years never out of widow's weeds. And so, every fourth Sunday, spring, summer, autumn, winter, come rain, snow, sleet, and sometimes shine, Matthew and I were excused morning chapel by our father and made to cycle with him over to the next valley to see her, four miles there, four miles back, Matthew's little legs furiously pumping away on his three-wheeler bicycle. But we never could decide which was the most punishing: Chapel? Or visiting *Nain* Frondeg? Nothing to do with the vagaries of the weather, or having to climb steep hills in both directions – what with cycling to and from school every day, we were well used to climbing hills and getting cold and wet. No, it was just that as young boys we couldn't understand why she always sat in her high-backed chair in a dark corner of her back room, dressed in black from neck to toes, buttoned-up black bodice and ankle length, black satin skirt, allowing glimpses of laced-up black boots, and a small, black bonnet on her grey head. We used to say she looked like "Old Mother Riley" (a comedy character, sixpence, from the old black and white film days) giggling, as children do, when whispering it (just between ourselves, that is, not to anyone else). But after seeing "Great Expectations" and realising why she was like she was, we called her *Nain* Haversham.

Her one constant companion was a wire-haired terrier that absolutely terrified us; his name was Jock. I've mentioned that Harrison, Ewen's and Jessy's bearded collie was eccentric. Harry was normal compared to Jock. Whenever *Nain* Frondeg had visitors – strangers or non-strangers, Jock didn't differentiate – the crazy animal used to tear around the room in some territorial circle, behind the sofa, under the table, across the hearth, snarling and snapping the whole time we were there. If we hadn't have sat with our legs under us, he'd have had our feet off at the ankles for sure. But *Nain* Frondeg wouldn't have a bad word said against him. Said it was us upsetting him, not him upsetting us.

The only time we looked forward to visiting her was when we knew my father's brother, Garwyn, was home. Fourteen years younger than my father, he was Lancashire's opening fast bowler and his claim to fame (no mean one, at that) was a wicket hat-trick against the touring Indian Test-team of the time. We called him Uncle "Ginnin", the name his county pals gave him. And on a par with Uncle Billy, he was our other hero.

He once bought *Nain* Frondeg a budgerigar. 'To keep you company,' he told her. 'What's more,' he added, winking at us, 'you can chat to it, budgies talk.'

'Birds talk!' she sniffed. 'Don't be silly, Garwyn. Since you left home I don't know where you get your ideas from, indeed I don't.'

On his next visit, she couldn't wait for him to sit down. 'That budgie, Garwyn!' she griped at him, 'It hasn't said a word to me.'

'More to the point,' Ginnin asked, 'have you talked to the budgie?'

'No, why should I?' *Nain* Frondeg retorted. 'I've been waiting for it to speak first.'

And to this day that's how I remember her, dressed all in black, living with a stressed dog and a dumb budgie.

But Ginnin and my father brothers? I never could understand such a difference between two siblings, and used to look for some sign of Ginnin in my father, but if it was there, I never saw it. To me, he was a stern, unforgiving man, for whom the only right way of doing things was *his* way.

But perhaps I shouldn't judge him too harshly. His climb up the ladder was a tough one. The eldest of seven children – four boys and three girls – he was only fifteen when his father died, and had to leave Grammar School to support the family. At that time this meant a local colliery. He worked there for thirteen years, until his other brothers and sisters were educated (*and* they all did well; two became hospital matrons) and only then did he take up accountancy, *his* chosen profession, studying well past midnight to do the five-year course in three, and passing every exam first time.

So, yes, maybe my remembrance of him is too hard? Certainly, years later when he retired and the stress seemed to seep out of him, he loved having Ewen and Carys for the day, he and my mother taking them out in the car – Chester Zoo being one of his favourites; the rack and pinion railway to the top of Mount Snowdon another, and if it was raining they all went to the cinema, choc ices, the lot. So, maybe there was a soft core there somewhere, but though I never saw it, I now had something to thank him for…

The inherent appendix that had given your Mummy – my all-in-all to me – early warning of the terrible C in her body.

I was even thinking kindly about him.

And looking forward to your arrival, Abigail, with new hope.

- eighteen -

'Isn't she gorgeous, Daddy?'

Carys was sitting in a wheelchair alongside me in the Special Care Baby Unit. She looked so pale…and so vulnerable. Knowing her well, the look in her eyes told me she had her fears; but she was keeping them to herself, stifling them, not wanting to be a burden.

You're not, Cara, you're not a burden. Never have been, nor ever will be, no matter what. But I know it's how you want to play it, so we'll all of us, Ian, myself; Ewen and Jessy; Anne and Tony – Meryn too, she says she wants to help as well – we'll all act out our parts and keep our own fears to ourselves.

As for Abigail Rachel Gannon, Guy Rankin was right. She was a real fighter, no disputing, pulling the breathing tube out of her nostril within hours of being placed in her incubator, letting us all know she could breathe on her own, "thank you, very much." And now, at only a day old, and weighing just 4 pounds 2 ounces, they were going to try feeding her by syringe instead of a drip. All this, as well as surviving her Mummy's operation.

'Yes,' I replied, looking down at my miracle granddaughter, wrapped in a shawl in my arms, and looking up at me with a fixed gaze – exactly like Carys, the day she was born, as if studying my face. 'She's absolutely beautiful.'

'Who do you think she's like, Daddy?'

(You of course, Carys. Identical.)

'I don't know, Carys, it's difficult to say when they're so small.' And she was, she felt so tiny in my grasp. 'A bit of you both, I suppose.'

'I think she has my eyes.'

'Oh, yes, she's definitely got your eyes.'

'It's too soon to say about the nose, but her mouth looks like Ian's.'

(What! those cute, bow-shaped lips? Oh, Carys, they're yours.)

'Yes, she's Ian there, all right, no doubt about it.'

'I'm so glad. She's the only one we'll have, so I want her to be both of us. Do you like her name?'

'It's perfect. She *looks* an Abigail. As for Rachel, Mum would have been thrilled. Thanks, Cara.'

'It was Ian. He was in such a good mood after she was born I took advantage and he agreed to it. I wish Mummy was here to see her.'

'I know you do, Cara. So do I. If you see Ian before I do, thank him from me.'

'I will, he'll be here about seven. Can I have her back now?'

I didn't want to let my precious bundle go, but…

I gently gave Abigail Rachel back. Carys took her and gazed down with such love at her baby daughter's face that it hurt to see it. As for Abigail, she seemed to sense she was in "my Mummy's" arms again and closed her eyes, as babies do when they feel warm and secure.

This hysterectomy has got to succeed. It just has to.

'Oh, I *do* love her, Daddy. Love her to bits. I'm so lucky, having three people to love so much. Ian, Abigail and you…And Ewen and Jessy, too. And Sara and Nathan.'

'No, sweetheart, *we're* lucky to have you. And I wouldn't like to tell you the state I was in, until I knew Abigail was in the clear.'

'Yes, isn't it wonderful. Our prayers answered.'

She waited for me to respond. I wasn't able to.

'Dad,' she confronted me. 'Why don't you try coming back to church—'

'I'll think about it, Carys.'

'Will you?' Carys persisted. 'Promise me you'll—'

I was saved by the arrival of a nurse with a small syringe full of milk. She gave it to Carys to hold, helped her gently place the nozzle between Abigail's lips, and slowly depressed the plunger for the liquid to be fed through a drop at a time.

Abigail seemed to jerk at the first drop, her eyes flickered open as if to say: 'Hey, this tastes good'. She certainly didn't need any persuading, closing her eyes again as if to appreciate it all the more.

Carys took over and throughout the feed, didn't once take her eyes off her baby. Looking down with such pride, such love, such adoration, at Abigail taking her milk, that again it hurt to see it.

I did something I'd stopped doing after the slow way Rachel died. Recently I'd been trying it again.

I prayed. Silently, within myself, so Carys couldn't hear me.

God, if you do exist, I'm begging you, as one father to another, please bring Carys safely through her operation.

And please, please, please make sure it's in time.

Abigail finished the milk, seemed to lift her head up for more…and burped…without being patted. At two months premature! Carys gave me the empty syringe and replaced the shawl about her baby's head, leaving only her tiny face to be seen. The nurse looked up from checking the dials on another incubator. Seeing the feed was over, she glanced at her watch and nodded to me with a smile, letting me know that Carys could have a little bit more cuddling time.

'Time.' The nurse had come up behind us without our noticing.

'Just another few minutes, Sylvia…please!'

'Sorry, Carys, but we have to think of you, as well. You need plenty of rest to get your strength back for the operation.'

Carys pretended to pout, then gently kissed Abigail Rachel on the forehead. 'Bye, sixpence,' she whispered as Sylvia took Abigail and placed her back in the incubator. Still unable to tear herself away, Carys tapped on the glass. 'See you later, precious, when Daddy gets here.'

Suddenly, out of character, she savagely jerked her chair about by its wheels. 'Back to my room, Dad,' she said abruptly, more as a command than asking me, yet with a catch in her voice, and as I was pushing her along the corridor back to the ward, she half turned her head, and on her cheek I saw wetness.

'Dad?' she said.

'Yes, sweetheart.'

'Everything will be okay with the hysterectomy, won't it? They'll catch the cancer in time?'

'Of course they will, Cara.' I gently gripped her shoulder. 'As Guy said, the appendix was a blessing in disguise. Pollyanna, Cara.'

Before gravitating to novels like *Pride and Prejudice*…and Mr Darcy…Carys's favourite was *Pollyanna*. Whenever things went wrong, she'd always try to find the bright side of the situation, asking herself what would Pollyanna have made of it.

'Yes, I know – Pollyanna…' but then she paused. 'Except…'

'Yes, sweetheart?'

'Please pray for me as well, Daddy?'

Oh, Cara, I never stop.

Not since that terrible day Guy Rankin told us.

I was still confused by it all.

Nor certain there was anyone up there listening.

Yet, deep, deep down in my soul, I never stopped.

- nineteen -

Both Ian and I gave Carys a hug.

She was sedated but still managed to squeeze our hands and give us a smile, then she was trolleyed away down the corridor to the theatre. Reaching the wing doors she gave us a final wave. And passed from our sight.

Ian and I went into the waiting room.

The next few hours were going to be the longest of our lives.

Ian crossed to a chair near the window and dropped into it, folded his arms across his chest as if shielding himself, and stared out over the fields at the sea in the distance.

I went to the drinks machine.

'Tea or coffee, Ian?'

Ian thought the chocolate tasted nothing like chocolate.

'Nothing thanks,' he said, keeping his back to me. Realising he wanted to be left alone with his thoughts, I chose coffee and sank into the nearest chair.

For me, it was evoking memories of Rachel being taken away for the same operation which was to be routine…

- twenty -

Just like Carys, Rachel gave me a sedated smile and a languid wave, then the corridor doors closed.

I sat in a waiting room chair with a book I'd brought with me – *Three Men In A Boat*, my favourite light-hearted read, to try to keep my mind occupied, but I couldn't concentrate, put it aside, and dug into my wallet for some photos of Rachel I always carried with me...

Remembering back to that time, Abigail, makes me think that maybe this is as good a time as any for me to tell you if only a little about your Gammy.

Especially as the top photo I was holding was one of her when she was only two.

Looking so much like Mummy Carys when she was also two.

And you, too, Abigail, when you were the same age.

It's hard to tell you all apart.

'When *we* have grandchildren,' Rachel used to say to me, 'I want to be called Gammy – *Nain* sounds old. And you can be called Gampy – *Taid* sounds old, too. And we're never going to be old, Luke, you and I.'

And being that much of your Gammy's blood flows through your veins, sixpence, helping to give you the will-power that was so evident in you from the very day you were born – two months premature but determined you were going to make it, and still shows itself, like when you're out playing and fall and hurt yourself, but you bite your lip instead of crying, and get back on your feet and carry on playing as if nothing has happened – this is another reason, as well as wanting to talk about her myself – for me to tell you a little about her.

And while I'm thinking about it, perhaps go just a little further back in time and also tell you something of this side of your family.

From where all three of you inherited your similar natures.

Starting with Rachel…

She was only twelve when I first saw her. The prettiest girl I thought then (and still do) I'd ever seen, all sun-tanned legs and open sandals in a short, dark blue gymslip, Italian-black hair and the deepest of brown eyes, on our first day at our new grammar school. Segregated, the boys' centuries old stone building on one side of a winding leafy lane, the girls' more modern one on the other, forbidden to even talk to one another without punishment – lines, detention, or three whacks – being meted out by lurking prefects eager to administer them, especially the whack.

But I was determined to know her name and paid a fellow pupil from her old junior school the then princely sum of half-a-crown (12½p) for it. Rachel. It so suited her. And on Valentine's Day, sent her a card with my *name* on it – not a question mark – via the same boy (he extorted another half-crown from me, the pimply chancer) and she replied with a pithy "get lost" note.

Still, relations of a sort had, I supposed, been established, and whenever I happened to see her after that, I'd wink at her and she would glower back.

And that's how the next six years passed…

Until we reached seventeen and after "matriculation" – "A levels" as it is now – we both left school, Rachel into the bank like her late father, a branch manager, who died of stomach cancer at only forty-one, when she was just twelve (the reason, her anger at life, as it later transpired, for her glowering at me when I winked at her – she'd not long been told he was so ill) and me articled to become an accountant like my father and inherit the family practice.

Both of us against our wishes.

Rachel wanted to study Fashion and Design at art college, I wanted to go to university to read English. But we both had bloody minded parents – me: my father; Rachel: her mother – who thought they knew better than us for us, and refused to listen to our pleas.

Yet, working in the same town our paths continued to cross, Rachel still staring me out in passing, until the day (still seventeen) when I finally plucked up the courage to stop her in the street and ask her to the cinema. To my big (*huge*) surprise she said "yes", and during the film whispered to me, *"What took you so long?"*

After that, our only separation was my two years in the army from the age of nineteen. In my day we had to give part of our lives to Queen and Country and dwindling Empire, and for me it was fighting parang-wielding communist guerrillas in the far-flung jungles of Malaya, guarding the incomes of faceless rubber plantation owners. As for those who, unlike me, didn't return – including my army pal Jimmy – but are buried out there in a distant land so far from home with no one to put flowers on their graves, it meant more than two years.

Rachel wrote to me every day I was away (apart only from when she was unable to for some reason – like the time she had a bad bout of flu) and we married a week after I arrived back in the UK to be demobbed (with me being overseas, Rachel made all the arrangements) both only just twenty-one, defying a concerted attempt to dissuade us by Rachel's mother and my father, who thought we were far too young to commit the rest of our lives to each other.

But commitment was mostly what marriage meant in those days, nor was there any trial living together first (well, hardly ever) and so…after four exceedingly prurient years of self control, with the last twenty-one months of it spent at opposite ends of the globe, thousands of miles apart from each other and missing each other like crazy, we could hardly wait to reach our London hotel…except, there waiting for us in the foyer was Aunty Gwenda–

But I've already told you this story, sixpence.

And hard though it is for me to keep it brief.

I'll return to life with Rachel…

The one thing certain about Rachel was her fiery nature which, though heaven for a lover, could sometimes – but only sometimes, and the other times were more than worth it

– make our life together somewhat…well, "lively" is as good a word as any.

Certainly it was never dull. And that, when I look back on it – which is often, oh, so very, very often – meant never boring, and there's one hell of a lot to be said for that..

I used to tease her it was the Jewish blood in her veins, which, despite her father's family being solid Welsh chapelgoers, she could hardly deny it – not with Uncle Moses, Uncle Aaron, or Aunt Rebecca popping in for tea and picking up Rachel's latest antique purchase to check its authenticity, especially if it was silver and had a hallmark – nor, for that matter, did Rachel want to deny it, and neither was *I* doing anything other than just ribbing her. When I was young, I used to dream of one day living on a *kibbutz,* helping the Israelites (as I thought of them) defend their rightful homeland. As for *Taid* Jonathan, Rachel's granddad – your great-great granddad, Abigail – he owned half the village they lived in. The shop that sold just about everything, the petrol station and garage next door, colliery, sawmills, bus service to the nearest town. All of which made him a self-made man of some success. Could anything be more Jewish than that?

His wife Elisabeth – *Nain* Bellis, Rachel's grandmother – stemmed from Italy, her family name "Belli" changed to "Bellis" when they fled to Wales centuries before to escape some then persecution of the Jews. I don't know the details, or from where in Italy (Florence, I think) but with "belli" being a genitive of the Latin "bellum" meaning "war", it added fuel to my teasing Rachel that it was more from this side of the family she'd inherited her *belli*cose nature. Except I didn't mean it, sixpence, really, it was all in jest.

Still, it was from *Nain* Bellis she inherited her Mediterranean looks. She had an old photo, all cracked and faded, of her *Nain* that she treasured, and they were as alike as two peas in a pod.

Nain Bellis died at thirty-two from ovarian cancer, leaving three boys and Aunt Gwenda – who was then just a baby. Jonathan was inconsolable and went into permanent mourning which lasted all of twenty years, sitting around the fire of an evening after work staring at a photo of her – the old faded one Rachel now had – the same expression of grief as my own *Nain* Frondeg, who wore widow's weeds for the rest of her life. If he could have worn sackcloth and ashes, he would have. Again, could anything be more Jewish than that? As for when he died – of a still broken heart, so it was said – at the age of only fifty-two, his estate was found to be at odds with the information he'd given over the years to the Inland Revenue. Despite his grief the old rogue had kept accumulating. I ask you, could *anything* be more…

But no, with a sneaking regard, and, I suspect, most everyone else's, getting one over on the taxman, maybe I'd best stop right there.

Except that by "getting one over" I should have said during his lifetime. The sad truth (at least for his four children, Rachel's father among them), was that what he won in life was lost in death and everything – properties, businesses, the lot – had to be sold off to pay his estate's huge back duties, and lashings of penal interest.

Rachel, in return for my teasing, would wrestle me to the floor and straddle me and thump me – thereby proving my point about the derivation of "Bellis" – all in fun, she'd say, with me holding up my arms trying to block her blows. Fun for Rachel at least, because she was proud of her blood ancestry, Jewish and Italian both. Welsh too – there was no one who cheered louder than Rachel watching Wales win at rugby on TV, especially against England – and the other national teams, too – except Italy, of course, she always kept a soft spot for them.

And so life continued, never, as I said, dull. Just recollecting it, Abigail, as I sat there waiting for Rachel to return from the operating theatre still brings tears to my eyes…

Hearing the ward doors open and trolley wheels approaching, I glanced through the waiting room window expecting to see orderlies with an empty one for the next patient, only to see Rachel on it, her face grey, still anaesthetized. They wheeled her into her room and the door closed.

Thinking how swiftly time had passed, I put my photos away and looked at my watch – and saw she'd been gone little more than half an hour.

And I knew. Without being told, I knew.

It's a strange and isolated feeling; more numbness than shock. You think you've made a mistake. Your watch has stopped. That modern techniques have maybe improved, and such operations are no more than taking a tooth out. But all the time you know, because a gnawing ache in your stomach tells you so. And so you don't move but just sit there, hoping it's a bad dream yet knowing the door will open any second, and a nurse who can't look you in the eye will come in and hold your arm ever so gently, and tell you the surgeon would like to see you when he gets back from theatre, but in the meantime…

Would you like a cup of tea?

Not coffee.

Or chocolate.

Just tea.

And then you *really* know.

Meanwhile, I sat there…and for some odd, almost detached reason, as if what was going on around me wasn't real, recollected articles I'd only casually read before, saying that cancer could lie dormant in someone for years, then something could just trigger it off.

With Rachel's sister, Helen, she first started feeling ill within months of her car being hit by a speeding old truck when she was travelling across Africa, and rammed over an embankment, ending upside down in a ditch. The truck driver sped off leaving her there, collar bone broken. It was five hours before another passing driver found her, lapsing in and out of consciousness, and drove her some thirty miles across bumpy dirt roads to the nearest hospital.

Helen was always convinced it was this that had started it. If so – and if my uneasy fear was more than just an uneasy fear – what could have triggered it with Rachel?

Could it be that time she kept me company as I built a new patio in the garden, sitting in a reclining chair chatting to me, while – unknown to us at the time – a cloud from

Chernobyl was hovering over us. Months later, in farms up and down North Wales, deformed lambs were born with two heads or six legs, and geiger counters checking the grass on which ewes were grazing, were going crazy trying to read the radiation levels. So, was it the Chernobyl fallout that caused Rachel to start feeling ill, I sat there brooding? Or as a TV documentary had suggested, could it have been triggered off by worry, or by stress?

Or maybe some bottled-up, inner unhappiness…

Because if anything had dominated Rachel's life it was this, stretching back to the death of her father when she was just twelve, and the apple of his eye. Almost every photograph of her childhood, each one treasured, told the same story: Helen, three years older than Rachel, holding her mother's hand; Rachel, looking cute with her mass of ringlets, always with her Dad. When he died, she was inconsolable for months, refusing to talk to anyone and playing truant from school, not wanting to hear other children talk about *their* dads. For me, as a husband, he was a hard act to follow…and I was never too sure I succeeded.

As for worry, particularly as to whether cancer was inherited in her blood, it had kept coming up in our conversations, even before we married.

Nain Bellis, dying at thirty-two.

Rachel's father, forty-two.

Helen, only thirty-nine.

To occupy her mind, Rachel kept moving us as a family. Eleven houses in twice as many years, all of them needing renovation or alteration, with Rachel helping the builders in every way she could, fetching and carrying and brewing cups of tea, making it seem as if we'd been sharing home with bricklayers and carpenters and plumbers and electricians and decorators for most of our married lives – until she fell in love with our present house and at long last we settled.

Happy years…

Then Rachel started to feel ill.

It got worse. A scan revealed ovarian cysts.

But nothing to worry about, we were told, they were benign.

All that was needed was a routine hysterectomy…

- twenty-one -

As I sat in the waiting room brooding at the closed door to Rachel's room, the gnawing in my stomach was getting worse by the second, when…

The ward sister entered, sat in the chair opposite me, rested her hand on my arm and told me that "Mr Wilford" would like to see me when he returned from theatre.

Meanwhile, Rachel was sleeping and wasn't to be disturbed.

And would I like a cup of tea?

And then I knew for certain.

I expected tears. When none came, I thought: What's the matter with me? Why can't I cry. But all I felt was disbelief. This couldn't be happening. It just couldn't. I was wrong. I had to be. Surely? Not Rachel?

Eventually, I was asked into Mr Wilford's room and told the operation had been aborted. The cysts were malignant, the cancer had spread, and Rachel had maybe four months to live. As I sat there, numb, he was called away to see Rachel, who'd woken up and was asking to talk to him on his own first, before seeing me…

I knew why.

She'd guessed.

And then I was allowed into her room.

Rachel was half-propped up by pillows and very pale, but she managed a smile and held out her hand. I took it and sat on the edge of the bed.

She searched my eyes, 'You've been told.' She always could read me.

'Yes, Rach.' At last I felt the tears well up, but I fought them. Rachel disliked weakness. 'But we can't give up, there's chemotherapy–'

'No, Luke, I don't want chemo. I saw what it did to Helen.'

(Helen fought it like a tigress for two years before the cancer won.)

'Mr Wilford says I've got four months. I'd prefer them to have some quality.'

'Rachel,' I protested, "you can't give up without fighting. I was reading only the other day of a new form of treatment. It's still experimental, but available if you can pay for it.' (I didn't say only in the USA.) 'I don't care what it costs, I'll find the money.'

'No, Luke, there's no point, it's too far advanced.' She took a deep breath, held it a moment before she was able to continue. 'I didn't tell you before, but the way I was feeling, I guessed what it was weeks ago. All Mr Wilford's done is confirm it.' She brought her other hand across and both hers held mine, 'There are only two things I ask of you…'

Her deep brown eyes held mine. I waited.

'I want to go at home, not in hospital, or a hospice. But most of all, I want *you* to look after me. A Macmillan nurse will be calling to see me, but I don't want a procession of others coming in and out.'

She gripped my hands. 'But above all else, I want you to promise to keep me free of pain.'

She searched my face. 'I know if you promise, you will. So, *promise me…*'

It was the way she asked it, more as a plea, that this time I was unable to hold back my tears. Rachel halted them with an admonition.

'That's another thing,' she said, 'if I'm to stay strong, you're going to have to be strong for me. That means no tears. What I want is for you to move our bed down into the den for me to be next to the downstairs bathroom and the sitting room just across the hall, with no stairs to climb, and make the house as inviting as you can for when I come home. Mr Wilford said two days.'

She gripped my hands again. 'Will you do that for me?'

I could only nod. I didn't dare try speaking.

'You've not yet promised no hospitals, no pain?'

'I promise,' I managed to say.

She let go my hands and stretched out her arms. 'And now that's settled I'd like a bear hug – a gentle one, don't forget the stitches.'

I leant over and held her. She clung to me not saying a word, then released me. There were tears in her eyes but I wasn't supposed to see them and said nothing. In any case, there was nothing I could say; she'd said it all, as usual.

'And now I'd like to sleep,' she whispered, closing her eyes tight.

And that's how I left her, with her eyes all screwed up, her face turned away on her pillow, and went home to make the house ready.

- twenty-two -

The day I brought Rachel home from hospital, a miracle happened.

When I set off earlier, I left a house full of welcoming flowers inside, and a garden looking beautiful, with new turf I'd had specially laid for her homecoming, replacing our old front lawn.

The hospital was only a mile away, so it was no more than an hour or so later that we were driving back down the hill. It was a beautiful spring day with the wide bay stretched before us, and the sun shining across its waters out of a clear blue sky, with but one wispy cloud in sight.

As we turned the corner and the house came into our view, we both gasped.

The new laid lawn was carpeted in yellow daffodils. Never had I seen so many clustered together, so thick we could hardly see the green grass underneath. To this day, I still find it hard to accept. The bulbs must have been in the fresh turf, yet only an hour earlier there was no sign of them. But it's exactly what happened.

'Oh, Luke,' Rachel exclaimed, transfixed by them. 'What a lovely welcome. It's just like in Wordsworth's poem – "when all at once I saw a host of golden daffodils". What a wonderful surprise; thank you for not telling me about them.'

'It's a surprise to me as well, Rach,' I said, hardly able to believe my eyes, and stopping the car to take it all in. 'An hour ago there wasn't one to be seen.'

She looked at me. 'You're not serious.'

'Never more so. When I left, there was only lawn.'

'Oh,' Rachel said, and for only the second time in my presence since being told she had such a short time to live, tears came to her eyes. But these were tears of joy not of sorrow, her face was all lit up. 'God's sent them as a sign. Of Spring. A new life. I felt at peace before and I certainly do now.'

'I'll cut you a bunch and put them in a vase in the den,' I said.

'No,' she protested. 'They're beautiful where they are. I'll be able to see them through the window. Let them live as long as they can.'

Let them live as long as they can. I can still remember her saying the words. So typical of her, especially then, with what she'd just been told.

'As for you and me,' she grasped my hand. 'Let's make the most of every precious second we've got left together. Bargain?'

'Bargain,' I said, and with her hand still on mine, I drove down the hill and into the drive.

We entered the house and it was almost as if you could touch the sense of peace inside. The den overlooked the bay and across to the Isle of Anglesey, and was big enough to take not only the bed but a settee, and a couple of armchairs I'd put in the window for us to sit and also see the Conwy estuary, and along the valley to the distant mountains of Snowdonia beyond.

I knew Rachel would like that. Her favourite psalm was:

I will lift up my eyes to the hills, from whence cometh my strength.

And that's how the four months passed; in peace.

I'm not saying there weren't times of sickness…and moments when she clung to me as though she didn't want to let me go…Nor am I saying she didn't deteriorate…she did, to when she wouldn't look at herself in the mirror anymore and I had to do everything for her, like gently brush her hair. And yes, I would sometimes catch her with moist eyes. But she never openly cried, oh no, not Rachel. I did that for us both. But only when her morphine dose put her into a deep sleep and she couldn't see or hear me to tell me off.

Yet, over all this, there was a pervading sense of peace.

The weather was glorious right through from April to early August. Carys was a rock, doing all the shopping, and we shared everything else: the cooking, washing, ironing. But we didn't vacuum, only dusted, we didn't want the intrusion of any harsh noises.

At that time, Ewen hadn't yet met Jessy. He'd not long joined the police after "escaping the boredom" of his bank job and was now a motorway "cop", loving every minute of it. And though he now had to live closer to his patrol station, he drove over every moment he could.

During the first months, while Carys was at work, Rachel and I would sit in the window and talk, mostly the "do you remember when we…" kind of talk, taking us right back to that first Valentine card I sent her when we were only eleven, and her pithy "get lost" reply; or we'd just sit silent, with me sometimes squeezing her hand to let her know how precious she was.

'What?' she asked me the first time.

'Does there have to be a what for squeezing your hand?' I asked back.

'Sometimes,' she answered. 'And that was a sometimes time.'

'I love you,' I said.

'Well that's all right then,' she said.

Her mother had died a few years earlier of pneumonia, and the only person she wanted to see – outside of myself and Ewen and Carys – was her younger brother, Simon, who lived sixty miles away and drove over twice a week. Nor did she want to see Aunt Gwenda (*'she'd only try to take over and boss me to think positive and get better,* Rachel said*, and I don't want all that'*) – or even my own mother, who was still living in her isolated home with no central heating, and still mowing the lawns and cutting the hedges. Despite them being the best of friends, she didn't want *Nain* to see her so looking so frail, knowing how much it would upset her, and I guess that was true. But I also suspect that seeing my mother – thirty years older than her, still sprightly and begging to come over to help – may have made her think of the unfairness of it all, and she didn't want that either.

She'd accepted what was happening to her…and she wanted it left that way.

But her decline of body was so rapid that when it came to bed-time — and so as not to hurt her should I tug the duvet if I moved — I pulled the sofa up to the bed and lay on it close enough to hold her hand. I only cat-napped and as we said our "goodnights" to each other she'd whisper to me in the semi-darkness: *"See you in the morning"*, and I'd say *"See you in the morning"* back. Later, these words were my dedication to her in my first novel.

Nor was there a day that went by without her telling me: 'I love you'. And reach out and clutch my hand after something I did for her, at times so small as to be trivial, but they seemed to mean so much to her. Later, as she got weaker and even frailer, and had to stay in bed more, she lost her voice, and her eyes would follow me around the room, forcing me to look at her, and she'd point to herself: *I*...cross her hands over her heart: *love*...and point to me: *you.*

It was as if she was seventeen again, and so was I to her.

And when she was asleep during the day, which was often now, I would sit alongside her and hold her hand, remembering back...

And as I looked at her sleeping face, so drawn now, yet to me still my beautiful Rachel, her dark hair flecked with grey, and her lips, their soft curve no longer full, but cracked with the effect of her medication, in their familiarity they were all restored to me, and I could see...

The eleven year-old girl in her gymslip who'd glared at me when I winked at her. If only I'd known then she was hurting, I would have smiled at her instead, to try to let her know that even though she thought her world had come to an end, it had not.

The girl's face fades…

To become that of a vivacious nineteen year-old, standing on the topmost platform of the Eiffel Tower, black hair blowing free in in the wind, and the skyline of Paris silhouetted behind her, allowed to be there by Rachel's mother only if we promised to "behave" ourselves (we did, and we did) to say our goodbyes to each other, the week before I went to Malaya.

It was another year and nine months to when I would see her again…

A young woman now, looking radiant in her tiered white lace wedding dress, walking down the aisle towards me on her uncle's arm, every feature of her lovely face clear to see because in her excitement she'd forgotten to lower her veil. And when we knelt side by side to receive our pastor's blessing, she squeezed my hand tight – and if ever a grip said 'I love you', that was it.

Oh, Rachel, 'I love you, too.' How could I not.

You were the most beautiful bride.

And the most wonderful mother…

I can still see the love in your eyes lighting your face as you gazed down at Ewen for the very first time, and the same look with Carys when – after the fight for your life had been won, but you were told you could have no more children – I put her in your arms to hold. Love mixed with almost disbelief that you'd still been blessed with the perfect family – a boy *and* a girl.

And despite all the worries that children bring, all the illnesses, all the ups and downs that life later threw at us, their childhood brought us so much joy and laughter.

Doubled-up laughter sometimes and often at me, like that time outside Tangiers when that camel I was trying to mount took an immediate and intense dislike to me, chasing me around the compound trying to bite chunks out of me as I leapt about like a jackrabbit, trying to avoid his champing teeth – and you and Ewen (but little Carys ready to cry, bless her) watching almost in hysterics.

At the time I couldn't make out how you found it so funny, but now, looking down at your sleeping face on your pillow, knowing I'm losing you and that we'll never share such moments again, well yes, I suppose it was.

And talking about such moments, those that stay engrained in memories, do you remember, Rachel, that time in Rome, all the fuss trying to get you inside St Peter's Basilica; turned away the first time because you were wearing tight black jeans (too sexy), the next day because your summer dress revealed too much of your shoulders, but after we finally made it inside – you now wearing my far-too-big-for-you summer jacket – its splendour was spoilt for you when we went outside again and you saw that legless beggar propelling himself about by flooring his hands on a wheeled trolley, pleading for alms, but being ignored by passing clerics.

'All the wealth we've just seen,' you said to me. 'But what use is it without the love.'

All the wealth...but without the love.

So expressive of the person you are, Rach.

Which was why you preferred the simplicity of your own personal faith.

Like the time spent walking the shores of Lake Galilee, imagining Christ fishing there and speaking to the multitudes, and – unlike those superior priests – feeding them loaves and fishes. And the hallowed sense of peace you felt at His simple tomb in the Garden of Gethsemane.

And the message you read in a cloud of golden daffodils, the day I brought you home.

Oh, my love, if there is a Heaven, you will be there.

But I'm going to miss you.

Really miss you.

- twenty-three -

Carys and I were with her at the end, holding her hands – Ewen was pacing the garden, too choked with emotion to be in the room.

Suddenly, Rachel smiled at someone in the corner of the room – someone Carys and I couldn't see – and in a voice no longer the hoarse whisper of the last weeks, she said:

'Yes, I'm ready.'

Then she turned to us: 'I have to go, there's a tunnel of light, and someone holding out a hand to me. Beyond it I can see the most beautiful colours. I love you both and Ewen. Tell him so. And look after each other, the three of you.'

She pulled a hand free and like a trusting child going for a walk held it out to someone in the alcove to hold.

'*See you all in the morning,*' she said to us.

And she closed her eyes and stopped breathing.

It was as peaceful as that.

I can't explain it, nor am I going to try, all I know is that for a split moment in time there, Carys and I were, in some small way, part of some awesome happening, a transition from this life to another, and that to have cried then would have been to negate the miracle of it. But on a human level, I just remember feeling relief that she was out of her suffering, and peace of mind that I'd kept my promise to her – no hospitals, no pain.

The tears came later that day when we opened her Bible at her page marker to see what she'd been reading. It was: *I will lift up my eyes to the hills, from whence cometh my strength,* and inside was a sheet of blue writing paper, simply addressed: *To My Family.*

Sitting together on the settee, with Carys in the middle, the three of us read her last words:

> *To my Belovèd Family*
>
> *I want to thank you for all your loving kindness.*
>
> *Who brings me a glass of water? Who brings me a cup of tea.*
>
> *Who brings me a beautiful meal and served so beautifully.*
>
> *Who shakes my pillows; who makes my bed?*
>
> *Who does the shopping? Who does my washing?*
>
> *Who lovingly touches me when I'm out of breath?*
>
> *Who cheers me with a smile?*
>
> *I just want to say thank you, you have been God's hands.*
>
> *I love you all so much.*
>
> *See you in the morning.*
>
> *Rachel & Mum*
>
> *xxxx*

It was then that we cried…

- twenty-four -

The sound of another trolley brought me back to the present. I had tears in my eye. I wiped them away and glanced through the window. The trolley had Carys on it. She was unconscious.

I looked up at the clock on the wall. And again, I knew.

A coldness came over me as I went through the same emotions I'd gone through with Rachel. My body felt the same numbness. But inside I was trembling. My heart and mind praying.

Oh, no not again! Please, not again, God! Not my precious Carys.

Ian was still looking through the window. I didn't say anything to him in case I was wrong. But deep inside me I had that dread feeling, and in my ear I could hear Rachel saying: 'If I'm to stay strong, you're going to have to be strong for me.'

Rachel had chosen not to fight, the strength she had wanted from me was to be with her through to the end. But Carys was young, with a life ahead of her, and Ian and Abigail to fight for...

And all the time as I brooded, the gnawing in my stomach told me I was right. Soon, all too soon, my beautiful daughter would be waking up to find the operation was too late. Instead of going home happy and smiling and all carefree to Ian and

Abigail, the nightmare over, and the life she'd always dreamed of stretched before her, just waiting to be enjoyed, she'd be going home to prepare herself to face chemotherapy…

But with the odds against her winning the battle considerably lessened.

Despite it all, she wouldn't give in. Oh, no, not Carys. I knew her too well. She'd fight.

She'd fight, tooth and nail. And she was going to come through it; damned if she wasn't.

I wasn't letting her go.

Are you listening, God? No way! Okay?

But if she was to win, she was going to need nursing…and caring…and all the help…and all the love…and all the strength she could draw on.

If I could have given my life for hers, I would. Willingly.

But as I couldn't, she had me for as long as it would take to beat it.

Six months?

Nine months?

A year?

Whatever. My writing didn't matter. Deadlines weren't important. Not compared to this.

What's more, if…*no*…*when* she won her battle, Ian must still have his job to provide for his family. As for Abigail, not yet out of the Special Care Unit but getting stronger every day, it wasn't going to be just "see you in the morning". At 4lbs 2ozs and needing constant feeding, it was going to be *see you all through the night* as well.

Yet I said nothing to Ian…just in case I was mistaken.

But if I wasn't, it meant telling Meryn we'd have to postpone once more. As this day had drawn nearer, we'd been so hopeful the operation would be in time we'd resumed our plans.

Would she again understand? Or this time was I asking too much? To again put her life on hold for…how long…

Maybe as much another year.

It was a lot to expect.

I reminded myself she was a compassionate person, Meryn. And all that mattered, all that was important, was Carys.

But it was still one hell of a lot to ask.

At that moment a young sister entered the room. I questioned her with my eyes. She wasn't authorised to say anything, but her own eyes, sad and kind of apologetic, said it all.

Ian looked up.

'Ian,' her voice was gentle. 'Mr Rankin is on his way up from theatre. Carys is back in her room. She's asleep, but he'd like to talk to you before you see her. And he suggests that maybe you'd like to have Carys's father with you? Meanwhile, would you both like a cup of tea?'

Ian's face went white, he remained silent, unable or unwilling to put his fears into words. I shook my head to the sister for the tea and waited for her to leave the room. Then I crossed over to Ian and sat opposite him.

'Ian,' I said. 'I wish I didn't have to say this, but I'm very much afraid you and Carys are going to be facing some big decisions. If so, I want to help. In any way I can…'

I clutched his arm. 'Maybe we should talk.'

- twenty-five -

Once again, I needn't have worried about Meryn's response.

'Of course I understand,' she said, tears welling in her eyes at my news. 'Oh, Luke, if it was me having to go through it, I'd have wanted my Dad's strength to help pull me through. We had the same relationship as you and Carys.'

She paused as the emotion of the moment caused her to remember her father. She'd shown me her photos of him, a happy good-looking man with the kindest of eyes. He was an architect, and it was Meryn who found him lying on her kitchen floor after a fatal heart attack – he'd only gone to make them a cup of tea, but he was gone so long she wondered where he'd got to, went to look and that's where she found him.

'If there's anything I can do to help?' she said, dabbing her eyes. 'Mum as well. We'll drive over as often as we can to see your mother for you, and take her out for lunch.'

'Thanks, Meryn,' I said. 'She'll enjoy that.'

And she would.

Other than my brother Matthew's and my weekly visits, my mother rarely saw much of anyone, living out in the country. She'd look forward to having Meryn's mum for company, she always did. With Welsh being their first language and their similar backgrounds, she would be in her element relating and – if Irwen could manage to get a word in

– listening to true-life stories, often hilarious, of Welsh village life from their youth.

I say "hilarious" and so they would be, knowing my mum and Irwen, but they also shared bitter experiences as children when, in their days, they were not allowed to speak Welsh – their own language – in school. Their punishment for being heard to do so, even at playtime – *and* between siblings who spoke only Welsh to each other at home – was a caning. Three of the best across each palm. It was an attempt by English authority to stamp out our language, and even in my day "Welsh" was still offered to us only as a "foreign" language. Today, things have changed, we now have our own schools with subjects taught in our mother tongue, and "English Language and English Literature" part of the curriculum. Sara and Nathan go to one.

But speaking of my mum, her father, Edward Rees – "Ted" Rees as he was called – was an overseer in a local colliery. Sadly, I never knew him – he was killed in a pit accident at the age of 43, before I was born – but she used to tell me about him, often with tears in her eyes.

His own father was gamekeeper to Lord Something-or-other, but Ted Rees had political ambitions. Forced to leave school at fourteen to look for work to supplement the family income (as it was back in those days) there was no choice for him other than be a miner. But he was determined to succeed and climbed his way up through the Miners' Lodge to become an impassioned open-air speaker for the then burgeoning Labour Party. A fire that was in his blood maybe?

Rees is a derivation of an Old Celtic word *ris*, meaning *a fiery warrior*…

Whatever, Ted Rees's oratory brought him to the notice of Labour's then Prime Minister, Ramsay MacDonald, and a dinner invitation to number 10 Downing Street, where he was well able to hold his own – and in appearance, too. I have a black and white photo of him standing outside the famous black door with my *Nain* Kate (Katherine) slim and elegant in a black velvet gown – a tall, handsome, dark haired, refined looking man, wearing a dark waist-coated suit with a gold watch and chain. And well able, I'm sure, to also hold his own in conversation, having educated himself in the evenings after coming home from the colliery, reading Dickens, Shakespeare, and other such writers (and the Bible, of course) all he could lay his hands on, far into the night, with only a sputtering candle for light.

He also paid for lessons on both the piano and violin, becoming accomplished on both, but it was the violin he loved best. My mother's great delight was when he'd creep up on Kate, especially if she was in the kitchen, covered in flour, making pies with fruit from their garden, apples, raspberries, rhubarb, or blackberries or whinberries picked wild – and play her romantic Italian music. However busy she was when he started, they would always end up laughing and hugging, and dancing around the room, the pies all forgotten.

Kate was Cornish – of Celtic origins, the same as the Welsh – and it's from her family we get our blue eyes. As for how it came about that Ted Rees, living in Wales – and Kate Harper, from Cornwall – ever came to meet, especially in

133

those days when 300 miles was almost like living on the other side of the world…

Well, it was that old Fate again.

Kate's father – my great granddad, James Harper – owned a tin mine in Cornwall, but when tin went into decline, he upped his family to North Wales to buy a lead mine instead. The one he chose (which happens to have a history stretching way back to Roman Times) was sited in the village next to Ted Rees's. I don't know how he and Kate Harper first met, or whether there was any initial opposition from Kate's father and mother to the match – them being "gentry" and Ted a coal miner – but I do know that from that moment there was no one else for either of them. Anyway, not only was consent given to the marriage, but realising how serious his new son-in-law was about his political ambitions, James Harper – to his credit being that he was a staunch Tory and a landowner, and Ted Rees of the new radical Party – bought them a large house on the edge of the village. Ted repaid James' faith by being chosen to represent one of the safest Welsh Labour seats as their candidate at the next general election. But then an underground truck jumped the rails one Saturday afternoon and he was crushed against the coal face; killed instantly. What's more, he shouldn't have been there. His brother, Tommy, had swapped shifts with him to sing at some *Eisteddfod* – a competitive festival of music and poetry, Abigail, common to Wales. Yet *another* example of how Fate can, and often cruelly, shape our lives.

When Kate was told how Ted had died, she went into instant shock and was paralysed from the waist down for the rest of her life. I was only a baby at the time and we went to live in *Nain* Kate's house for my mother to look after her. She used to nurse me in her bed to give my mother a break. I was her first grandchild and according to Uncle Billy a bit of a "bawler". So, *poor Kate,* having me to put with on top of not being able to walk.

Billy, as I've already mentioned, was Matthew's and my other hero along with Ginnin, and on one long-talked about occasion, playing for Wales's amateur football team, scored all five goals against an England eleven, earning himself the nickname, which stuck to him all his too short life, of *"Billy Rees Pum Gôl".* He was only sixteen when I was born and still living at home. But it was Billy who always got up to me in the night when I cried; my mother – who went suddenly deaf at the age of seventeen and had to give up going to university – never heard me, and my father *never* got up, swearing blind he'd slept like a log and hadn't heard a thing.

I loved Billy and always turned to him, rather than my father, in times of trouble, but then he was killed at the age of only twenty-six when some scaffolding (he was a builder) collapsed on him. I missed Billy terribly after he was gone. As for *Nain* Kate, she didn't live long enough for me to know her, but died when I was a year old, and we stayed living in the same family house James Harper built, and where Matthew, my brother, was born.

We loved it. When we were children it was surrounded by open fields and woods where we roamed being Robin Hood with bows and arrows we made ourselves from saplings, and at other times Zorro, wearing cloaks and masks made for us by our mam, but it's now encircled by an estate of newly built red-roofed bungalows, and somehow looks lost.

Incidentally, sixpence, regarding our Cornish roots, I once researched our family tree, and back in Kate's is a John Opie, whom I discovered to be a famous artist, with such a natural talent that by the age of only nineteen he was being called "The Cornish Wonder Boy"; and of whom it was once said, by Lord Northcotte, that while "other artists paint to live, Opie lives to paint."

Born 1761, we're descended from him through his favourite sitter, a pretty milkmaid named Mary James, whom he was going to marry. When he journeyed to London to seek his fame he left her behind, only nineteen, not knowing she was pregnant. Years later he wed the novelist Amelia Anderson, yet for the rest of his life he kept in his studio a picture he'd painted of Mary.

Known for his oil portraits and depictions of historic scenes, one, *The Assassination of David Rizzi*, a dramatic study, hangs in London's Guildhall Art Gallery. A great friend of Joshua Reynolds (who described him as "Caravaggio and Velasquez in one") he was appointed Professor of Painting at The Royal Academy of Art, but died at 45, and is buried next to Reynolds in the crypt of St Paul's Cathedral. Your Uncle Matthew is also an artist, Abigail and he reckons it's from John Opie he's inherited his talent. Possibly, but if painting *is* in the blood, then if I was Matthew, I'd check whether Pollock is also related to us. Not that I don't like my brother's work, I do, one of them hangs up in my study. It's great, full of colour. I'm looking at it now, and also at a photo of *The Assassination of David Rizzi*, and I still reckon Matthew's more Pollock than Opie.

When you're a little older, Abigail, perhaps you and I can go to London together to see John Opie's epitaph, and maybe ask him why he never came back for great-etcetera Grandma Mary?

But back to Meryn, my mother loved seeing her. If ever I drove over on my own without her, I'd get a ticking off. Whereas, if Meryn was with me, my Mum's face would light up. Hugs from two people she loved. Much better than just one – double ration.

I miss her, my mother, there was so much love in her, it was so much part of her nature – her family's, too, all of them so affectionate, uncles, aunts, cousins – I like to think I take after them; this is why, when I started writing, I changed my name to Rees.

My mother, I think, was secretly pleased.

'I like Meryn,' she said to me when I drove over one day to take her out for lunch. 'I hope you'll both be very happy together.'

'We will,' I told her.

- twenty-six -

I put my writing aside and went to live with Carys, to care for her and Abigail.

And six months passed.

Carys was away on her last chemotherapy.

I was expecting her and Ian home any minute.

And like the trooper she'd always been, she was winning her battle.

But that was Carys, a real fighter if ever there was one. I was so proud of her, so very, very proud, and so full of relief that the tension of the last six months had almost dissipated.

Almost…

Before Carys started medication her cancer count was high. But after the first treatment it halved, the same with the second, and the third, and the fourth. While she was away, she'd have been told the result of the fifth and if that had halved as well (*which it had to do, pray it hadn't stayed the same*) she'd know it was in retreat. There would be only the result of the sixth left (the one she was away from home on now) and if that also halved, it would be back to being as low as for everyday people who didn't have this terrible disease…

And the battle would be won.

Don't misunderstand me, the going had been anything but easy, and particularly cruel for Carys, who was the one having to go through it all. Ian too, he'd stayed strong. I was proud of him as well…and grateful beyond measure. So young, only twenty-three, hardly married, yet having to go through all the trauma of it. But he'd never cracked, supporting and encouraging Carys throughout, especially when she was feeling at her illest and low in spirit.

As for me, watching the daughter I'd once held as a baby in my arms, only one minute old, and had promised her that no harm would ever come to her, not if I could help it…well, it had been tough. And unable to put it all right for her, like when she was a child and fell over and hurt herself and I would "kiss it better", had just made me feel worse, and so…so helpless.

But we'd had plenty of support from everyone who loved her – a list as long as my arm – especially Ewen and Jessy, Ian's mother, Anne, and his sister Donna.. Together in the sitting room in the dusk of the evening, with the door closed for Carys not to hear us from the bedroom, we'd all of us often cried. Tears for every emotion, even *anger* at seeing what the treatment was doing to her, the appalling sickness which lasted for days after each session, the terrible loss of weight, her hair falling out – though she did look kind of cute after giving herself a close-crop one day in an effort to halt it, all sort of a young Sinead O'Connor.

'Think I'll keep it this way when it's over,' she jested, looking at herself in the sitting room mirror. 'It highlights my eyes.' Except that was said in defiance, because they now looked like dark pools in her pale, translucent face.

But then came tears of relief that her count was coming down. Then tears of joy from knowing she was winning, that this…*this cursed…malignant thing* , wasn't just in retreat, it looked as if it was licked.

Yet, the particular treatment she was on was so damned harsh, so distressing, that knowing she was winning was the *only* good thing about it. I'd seen its effects on Helen, Rachel's sister, and that was bad enough, but seeing it on one's own daughter was infinitely worse.

Knowing she'd sometimes wake up in the middle of the night, feeling poorly, and come through on her own into the sitting room for Ian to be able to sleep on, I'd leave notes for her on the arm of her chair. Short notes, nothing maudlin, to let her know I was there for her should she need me for company, whatever time of the day, or night.

To which she would always reply, and leave them in the same place – our postbox, as it were – reassuring me she was okay, like the one I keep with all the others in my desk drawer (I'll just get it)…saying:

> *4.15. Don't worry Dad, had a wonderful deep sleep for a few hours & feeling very refreshed. Now going to make myself a mug of warm water with glucose and take a pill, then going back to bed for another couple of hours. But I want you to know how nice it is that you are here. It makes me feel safe.*
> *Love U, Carys, xxx*

Even though it's just a note, it tells of her unique spirit and courage.

Nevertheless…

Seeing her so thin, so frail, sometimes hardly able to walk, made me literally weep inside, one minute wanting to break everything in sight, the next wanting to *cwch* her in my arms – the way I used to all those long years ago – and whisper to her not to worry, that everything would be all right, because I would see to it.

Except I couldn't, I was powerless, and that just made me so…so *bloody angry* again.

But Carys wouldn't want me to dwell on that side of it; not even the twice I had to tear down the motorway at way over the speed limit, Abigail in a baby seat in the back. Both times caused by the treatment. The first time in agony with kidney stones. The second time when I found her comatose in bed and had to carry her to my car and strap her in. Safely in hospital, it was found her potassium was so low she could have faded away in her sleep.

But I know Carys would prefer me to talk of the positive, so I will…

In which case, there we were, Abigail and I, sitting on the veranda, waiting for Carys and Ian to come home. It was early August, Carys's birthday was only ten days away, I was hoping the warm weather would last. It was holidaymakers' time, the ancient Norman castle of Conwy was standing tall in the distance and the tide was in, filling the estuary, fishing boats and yachts were bobbing about on its surface, and a heat haze was shimmering up from the motorway curving its way between green fields toward a new tunnel under the river, giving the speeding traffic a rippled effect. The cars and

141

coaches looked like miniatures moving without any engine noise, only the combined swish-swish-swish of tyres drifting up to where Abigail and I were sitting.

The weather had been like this for weeks now and Abigail's skin was lightly tanned. She was also getting chubby, in an oh-I-could-squeeze-her sort of way, and at six months old she'd caught up so much, no one would ever guess she was born five weeks premature.

I'd dressed her in a shell pink frock Meryn had bought her. She looked – well, I could eat her, sitting back in one of those canvas recliners on a metal frame, deeply concentrating on the fluttering flight of a multi-hued butterfly. It suddenly decided to meander away. Abigail turned to look at me and smiled, then proceeded to tell me what she was thinking.

'Ga-ga-ga,' she intoned, and I knew exactly what she meant.

'Yes, precious, pretty colours.'

'Ga-ga-ga.'

'Yes, sweetheart, Mummy and Daddy will be home soon.'

Another lovely smile, then she continued our conversation.

'Ga-ga.'

'Yes, darling, Gaga thinks you look really pretty in pink.'

I'd decided I was going to be called "Gaga", not "Grandad" – and certainly not *Taid*. Ewen and Carys had called my father *Taid*, which ruled that out for me. As for "Grandad", I thought it sounded old – shaggy grey hair, bowlegs and a gnarled stick – and although Sara and Nathan called me "Gampy", Abigail was making it clear that *her* name for me was to be "Gaga".

'Ga-ga.'

'Yes, baby. Mummy and Daddy will think you look pretty, too.'

'Gaga.'

'No, I know you can't wait to see them, sweetheart. And they'll be aching to see you, too…Sorry, I didn't catch that…No, they won't be long now. It's almost three o'clock.'

She was a real joy to us, a really happy baby which is what we needed at a time like this, cheering those low days for us, and most importantly giving Carys so much joy – and especially giving her the strength to get through the first week after each treatment, when the going was really tough.

Her treatment was every third week. At these times, Ian was given four days off work, two to take her to hospital – a specialized unit, all of fifty miles away – staying overnight; and two at home nursing her, which were Carys's worst days. Then it was back to his work for Ian, six days a week, leaving at seven in the morning, and returning about seven in the evening, even later on Tuesdays with all the stats to be faxed to Head Office.

By then, Carys was over the worst, and I was able to nurse her as well as look after Abigail. Mind you, those first few months were quite…well, hectic was putting it mildly. With Abigail at only just over 4lbs, and needing changing, feeding, burping…changing, feeding, burping…changing, feeding, burping…in an almost around-the-clock routine, with hardly any dozing off time – and Carys to be cared for, as well.

It cut out all thought of editing *The Celeste Conspiracy*, but I

143

didn't regret it, in the real world what did any of it matter compared to getting Carys well.

Abigail soon cut out the two-in-the-morning feed. As for Carys, after three days in bed following each treatment, she was able to get up and join us in the sitting room for a couple of hours at a time. Her great pleasure was after I'd fed Abigail and she'd take her "sixpence" in her arms to hold. Heartbreakingly, for no more than five minutes because her treatment left her weak, and as tiny as Abigail was, she was too heavy for Carys to hold any longer than that. It was tiring, often exhausting, but the look of love on Carys's face as she *cwched* her baby was a joy to see, and made it all the more worthwhile.

Anne came to relieve me one evening a week, and stayed the night to do the 6am feed, as well. Tony, Ian's father, drove her over and went straight back home. But he wasn't able to make it until after eight, and so, by the time I'd have showered and changed, the evening would mostly be over, certainly too late to see Meryn, and I therefore had an early night and a morning lie-in until eight, when Tony returned to drive Anne to work.

Donna did another evening. She worked only a mile away, arriving good and early about six, which meant that this and Ian's day off work, enabled us – Meryn and me – to have two evenings a week together.

If she was in, that is…

Recently, rather than be "stuck in the house on my own", she'd picked up again with her best friend Gaenor.

And if she *was* in, then if she wasn't too tired.

144

'Today's been hectic in the office, I think I'd like to have an early night.'

'You mean even earlier than your usual nine-thirty?'

'Yes, do you mind? I'm shattered.'

'We don't have to go out. I could pop over, if only to say hello?'

'It seems hardly worth it for only two hours.'

'Yes, maybe you're right. Have a good night and hopefully see you next week. I love you, Miss Asher.'

'Me too,' she'd say. 'Good night.'

And so I'd go to bed early and be asleep five minutes later, almost as soon as my head hit the pillow.

Still, Meryn was "thrilled" that Carys was getting better, and regularly sent flowers.

Ian's car came around the corner.

I picked Abigail up. 'See, didn't I tell you? Here's Mummy and Daddy.'

Abigail studied the car, her face somewhat bemused. I held her chubby wrist and helped her to wave.

Carys was lying back, the seat half down. Ian freed one hand from the steering wheel and raised the seat to help her sit up. She looked even paler than usual but waved back…then gave a smile which lit up her face and put her thumb up.

Her count had halved. My heart leapt.

Bless you, Carys, you're a real fighter; a real fighter, all right.

They turned into the driveway. Being a split-level house, they were below us. Ian hurried to Carys's door and helped her out. They both looked up at Abigail and me on the

145

veranda. Carys smiled again, but nothing more. After the chemo and long journey, she never had any strength in her voice to call up.

Abigail recognised them and shouted.

'Hello, sixpence,' Ian responded, being Carys's voice for her, using her name for Abigail, then put his arm around Carys and supported her to the front door.

I carried Abigail indoors and across the sitting room to the top of the stairs, to wait for the chair-lift (specially installed) to bring Mummy up to us.

After her treatment, Carys never came too near Abigail, wanting to safeguard her from any form of associated danger, and just stretched out a hand to squeeze her "sixpence's" plump little hand. Ian always gave Abigail a hug and a kiss, then took Carys to their bedroom, settled her head into her pillows and tucked the duvet around her, and stayed with her until she fell asleep. He'd then come through to be with Abigail and sit cuddling her in his favourite chair, enjoying every moment with her, just unwinding after the strain of the last thirty-six hours.

But today, when they reached the top of the stairs, Carys squeezed Abigail's hand as she always did, then with tears in her eyes held out her arms to me, wanting to be hugged. Ian had tears in his eyes, too. He took Abigail from me, leaving me free to hold my precious daughter.

Carys *cwched* into me, and held me as tight as she was able to. I returned it as closely as I dared without hurting her, she was so frail.

'Daddy, we're winning,' she whispered. 'The last count was

halved. If this one comes through as halved too, it will all be over. Won't that be wonderful?'

'Wonderful,' I said, gently stroking her tightly cropped head.

She kept clinging to me, the relief pouring out of her.

It seeped out of me, too. I felt ashamed of all my doubts.

Yes, Cara, we're winning, I thought.

Just one more count to go.

- twenty-seven -

The count came in, it had halved. Carys now needed to have only monthly check-ups.

After our tears of joy, Carys first thanked God, and then we made phone calls, too many to list. And when they were over, we decided on a celebratory party at *Plas-ar-Hendir* to share our happiness with the same close friends and family we invited to Carys's wedding reception.

It was also an opportunity to celebrate Carys's birthday; she'd be twenty-nine on the day. Her hair was starting to grow back, but only a dark shadow, and she bought a new wig for the occasion – the latest style, very glamorous, and *very tawny*, "to give me a boost".

She'd lost even more weight, but her make-up hid her paleness and she looked beautiful – in an ethereal sort of way.

'Julia Roberts, eat your heart out,' she said to her mirror reflection. 'Count yourself lucky I didn't audition for *Pretty Woman* – you'd never have got the part.'

Later that week, driving Meryn to the celebratory party, with her sitting beside me in the front seat, it felt just like a first date again.

'This feels just like a first date,' I said to her.

'And perhaps you and I can now get back to normal living,' she said.

Back to normal living, did I hear Meryn say?

Eight weeks later the pain was back, Carys's cancer count shot back up, and she started a new course of chemotherapy, a new treatment. I can't remember its name, only that it was the same experimental drug I'd wanted Rachel to have, and was being hailed as a miracle cure.

I can also remember praying for it to work a miracle on Carys.

Knowing that if it failed, there was nothing else anyone could do.

Speaking for myself, it felt as if we were being played with like yo-yos.

One minute, up; next minute, down.

Up, down…up, down…

Not knowing when or where it would stop.

But despite all my doubt, all my perplexity, I continued to pray.

Out loud on my knees in the privacy of my bedroom at night.

Silently in my heart and soul during the day.

Saying…*I no longer know what words to use, God, or how else to beg, but please let my precious daughter live.*

Ian needs her so much.

So does Abigail.

And God, so do I.

Meanwhile, we were back in the same routine, living one day at a time, from one session of chemotherapy to the next, except this new treatment was kinder than the other, with very little sickness and that was soon over, letting Carys enjoy every precious moment she could with Abigail. To be able this time have her "sixpence" on her knee, to kiss and to cuddle her, looking at her with such love as if hardly able to believe she was for real, and so absolutely perfect in her eyes, "the prettiest, bestest, preciousest" baby ever.

As for when Abigail fell asleep in Carys's arms and I had to carry her to her cot, it was only with the greatest reluctance that she let her go. I had to almost prise her away.

Then came the first result.

The count had halved.

In which case, then surely – with this being the "miracle drug" that Carys and others like her had long been waiting for – this surely gave more than a hope, more a promise really, that it – IT, the evil invader – could be beaten?

We waited, hardly daring to believe, for the result of the second count.

Finally, it came.

It was halved.

And once again our spirits rose, rose up on high as if to join the nightingale in its song.

Now Mummy's delight in you, Abigail, knew no bounds.

She enjoyed every single moment, every waking second of your progress. Watching you struggle to crawl, and you looking so puzzled at the cheers from her and Daddy – and me too – the day you first made it, wondering what all the fuss was about. Then your face smiling back at us, realising you must have done something smart. "Aren't I clever?" your cute expression seemed to say.

But before then came the "da-da" and "ma-ma" stages, with Daddy and Mummy wanting to believe you knew what they meant. You soon cottoned on to that, realising that in some way the sounds were pleasing them and kept repeating the sounds for their entertainment, with a really wicked grin on your adorable face.

Oh, Abigail, I hope you never change. You'll probably grow up to be an actress, the many ways you milked our applause.

I can still remember the first time you stood up, gripping your playpen rails and rocking at your knees until they gave in and you collapsed plonk down on your Teddies, then straightaway pulled yourself back up, and we knew we wouldn't have too long to wait for your first steps.

From then on there was no holding you back, you were literally "into everything." I've never known such a busy, yet contented baby. I'm sure you will have seen yourself in all these different stages on the videos Daddy took of you; but you were special, really special.

Unique.

To Mummy and Daddy, at least.

And to me.

If it was possible, the more you progressed, the more Mummy loved you; hardly able to believe there could be such perfection. "My precious little sixpence," as she called you, often with tears in her eyes, she loved you so much, and wanted so much to live for you.

Soon, she was strong enough to drive her vroom-vroom car again – with Daddy or me for company to make sure she was okay – and push you for short journeys in the buggy about town, hoping to bump into someone, *anyone* she knew, especially one of her friends, to show you off to. And, oh boy, when she met one – did she know how to show you off.

So much did she improve that she and Daddy decided to take you on holiday – two weeks at a favourite and secluded hotel of ours near Torquay in Devon, with its own stretch of beach, no doubt to enjoy making castles in the sand with you.

And build castles in the air too, I shouldn't wonder, because her last count had come through, it was also halved, she had only one left, and if that halved as well…

We could really hope again.

- twenty-eight -

When Carys told me they were going away, I phoned Meryn for her to pack her cases to fly off with me to Italy. Sorrento, I thought, where we spent our only holiday together, to rekindle the romance that had had so many ups and downs, so many highs and lows.

But all I got was her answer-machine and had to leave a message.

She returned my call the next day to say that Gaenor had sprung the same brief notice on her, and not knowing I would be free she'd pretty well said "yes". They were thinking Tuscany, she needed the break, she said. So I replied: 'Then you must go. Make sure you send me a card.'

She did – it arrived when Carys, Ian and Abigail were in Devon – posted from Lake Como. They were also planning two days window-shopping in Milan (said the card) and an open-air opera in Verona, but otherwise she was lounging around the hotel pool, recharging her batteries.

Since Carys started her second course of chemotherapy, we'd seen even less of Meryn than before. After sympathising when I told her that Carys was having to have further treatment, she made a suggestion to relieve me of all the pressure.

'You know I'd like to help, Luke,' she said, 'but I think the best way is to leave you free to look after Carys. She's going to need all your love and attention to see her through this new treatment. Perhaps it would be more sensible if I took a back seat for a while? Should you feel like a change now and then, you know where I am. But phone first,' she added, 'to make sure I'm in, though there's hardly a moment when I'm not thinking of you all.'

So, on the evenings I was free – before she went to Tuscany, and after she got back – I would phone first. But again it was that message-machine I'd get, and by the time she'd return my call after getting back from Gaenor's – or her mother's, or one of her other friends – I'd long been in bed reading. And after exchanging "hellos" and "how-are-you", we'd say "goodnight", hoping for better luck next time.

I must confess that I started wondering about all the people she was visiting.

Was she using them to avoid me, or simply not picking up the phone, not wanting to tell me – with all I was going through – that it was all over between us?

Or was she seeing someone else?

Was it really Gaenor she went to Tuscany with…

But all these doubts and questions went out of my mind the day Carys came home sobbing from her final treatment.

The count hadn't halved, it had doubled.

There was nothing more the hospital could do.

She was now in the laps of the gods.

Or just one?

I now started brooding…how would I cope if I lost her? She was everything to me, how could I live without her? Would I *want* to live without her?

I thought of all the different ways that others in our family had reacted to grief.

Nain Kate shocked into paralysis on hearing that Ted Rees had died so cruelly down the coal pit.

Nain Frondeg becoming *Nain* Haversham-in-black, cutting herself off from the rest of the world in her high-backed chair in the darkest corner of her sitting room, with only a dog and a budgie for company.

Rachel's *Taid* Jonathan, pining for his Elisabeth for all of twenty years.

And her other "Gamps", old Ethan Shaw (no, I've not mentioned him before) who hacked down his wife's, Mary's, cherished hydrangeas, twenty or more, a glorious display of blues and pinks, just because he couldn't bear the thought of anyone else touching them. He regretted it the rest of his life, but in that one moment, in the extremity of his grief, he cracked.

That's what grief can do.

And so we waited, keeping our inner fears to ourselves, yet it was there nonetheless, all three of us with our own inner dread, yet hoping, still hoping, for a miracle to happen, living each day at a time.

That was all we could do.

- twenty-nine -

It was mid-September.

The patio doors were open wide on to the garden for us to enjoy the late Indian summer. Carys was kneeling on the sitting-room carpet, happily playing with Abigail, who was now nineteen months old, and more and more confirming herself as a busy bee, cute, with an infectious grin, and as bright as a button.

Their laughter was wonderful to hear.

Carys's so full of joy, Abigail heartily chuckling at everything Mummy was doing. Maybe the miracle was going to happen, after all. Carys's hair was growing fast again, thicker and curlier than it was before. She might be a wife and a mother, but to me she was…well, she was still my daughter…and my pal. As for Abigail, I just adored her, and also had a sense of…of pride almost, that I hadn't made a bad job caring for her, and given her lots of fun, too.

And typical of children, it was the simple pleasures that gave her the most enjoyment.

Riding on the double-decker bus to town, especially the top front seat, instead of by car.

Going up and down…up and down…up and down… never fewer than five times…the escalators in Marks and Sparks, and never seeming to tire of it.

We understood each other so well that–

Carys grimaced and clutched her stomach.

'Daddy, I'm not feeling well.'

She looked up at me, her eyes full of pain.

Not only physical pain, but also the pain of fear.

And locked there in the fear, I could see the pain of certainty.

'Help me to a chair, Dad,' my precious daughter whispered, not wanting Abigail to sense, as children do, that something was wrong.

My heart gave a lurch. She hadn't needed help for months now.

I lifted Abigail into her play-pen amongst all her dolls and things. She fell back on to them, rubbing her eyes, suddenly tired and *cwched* a big yellow Teddy. She'd soon be fast asleep.

Turning to Carys, I helped her to a chair. 'Exactly what do you mean – don't feel well?' I asked, propping cushions around her and trying to hide the anxiety in my voice. 'Maybe it's something you've eaten?' But I was dreading her answer. She'd been looking paler and more hollow-eyed recently, but I'd not said anything – just prayed I was mistaken.

'No,' she grimaced as another spasm hit her, 'I feel ill, Dad. It's been coming on for a while now. It started with niggling pains and I was hoping it was something else. But today…' she choked on her words, 'I've got real pain, Daddy. It's back.'

She burst out sobbing. I knelt and held her until she'd expended herself. Then I felt her stiffen her back. She pulled away, dried her eyes, then spoke in a controlled way that was all the more anguishing because I knew she was putting it on for my sake. She was such a gutsy tinker, this daughter of mine. But, oh, how I wished she didn't have to be. Why in the hell has it had to come back?

Why couldn't it damn well leave her alone?

'This time it's not going to go away,' she said. 'Will you phone Ian? I'd like him to come home. But before he gets here, take Abigail for a walk. I'd like to be alone to tell him.'

I wanted to cry buckets. But then I heard Rachel's words. *If I'm to stay strong, you're going to have to be strong for me. That means no tears.*

And so, before phoning Ian, I gave Carys another hug, holding her tight and stroking her soft new curls, her head buried in my shoulder, her arms clinging oh-so-very-tight around my waist as she rocked herself against me.

But still no tears from me. I could cry later. Under the blankets in the privacy of my room, so no-one could hear me.

She was right. She knew the pain. New tests showed that her blood count was back to being high – very high, and no further medication could help.

Only that bloody miracle.

But if it was going to happen it had only four months, the time they now gave her.

Four months!

Even now, when I sit alone in my study, or out on the patio in the fading light of evening, looking down the estuary at the darkening mountain peaks pointing up to the star-flecked sky, I still relive the terrible finality of those words.

Oh, Carys, Carys.

Ian asked for time off work and was given it. As for me, I knew I was losing a daughter and I've already told the agony of that. But my heart went out to him. Here he was, not long married and thinking that the whole of their life together was in front of him and his "Cris". Instead of which, he was soon, and so very young, going to be left alone with a baby daughter to bring up.

I kept looking at him, trying to guess his private thoughts. If only I knew, I might be able to help him. He was suffering, I could tell by the look in his eyes. But as always, Ian kept his thoughts to himself and so I didn't ask. Just told him I was there for him. That I'd been through what he was going through, and though I'd been nowhere near so young losing Rachel, I knew the pain of it, and should he ever need a shoulder to cry on…

But Ian kept it all bottled up inside him. I knew that's what he would do.

And so we settled, the three of us, to try to live our lives as normally as we could, praying – in which I now joined in as never before – that prayers would succeed where medicine had failed, and we would be granted that miracle. Making Abigail the centre of our focus, trying to enjoy each day as it came.

Yet all the time it hung there.

Like a black shadow hovering over us.

I no longer went out, not even for a newspaper. The world and all its problems could go by as far as I was concerned.

I wouldn't have my daughter for much longer.

Every moment was precious…

As for Meryn, I just hoped she would understand.

But she'd become even more distant lately – if that was possible. I kept inviting her around, to be part of us some evenings, especially when Ewen and Jessy were coming over. Carys even phoned her herself, saying she'd love to see her. And knowing how private a person Meryn was, how much she disliked revealing her emotions to others, invited her to come, if she preferred, when no one else was calling, and they could chat together as they used to, just the two of them.

But Meryn again said she didn't want to intrude on us as a family, yet was always thinking of us. Except that not wanting to see Carys – and Carys so ill, and sinking visibly – it hurt bad.

Real bad.

But then one day, halfway through the four months they'd given her – Ian and Abigail were out shopping, then calling to see Anne and Tony and so wouldn't be back for hours – Carys came through to the sitting-room (I thought she was sleeping in her bedroom) and said:

'I've called the ambulance, Dad. It will be here in ten minutes. I phoned the local cottage hospital last week, they said they'd keep a bed for me in a room on my own, just like a hospice. I've also packed my bag. Will you carry it down for me?'

It was all so sudden, so out of the blue, she'd not even hinted at it, the only thing I was able to say was:

'But Carys, shouldn't you wait for Ian to get back, first?'

'No, I'm doing it now, while he and Abigail are out, he'd only try to stop me. But after seeing it with Mummy and knowing what the next few months are going to be like, I don't want them to have to live with it every day, like we did. It wouldn't be fair on them. If it was only Ian and no Abigail it would be different, but I don't want him to have me to nurse as well. After I've gone, he's going to have to bring Abigail up on his own, it will be good for him to be alone with her, she's so used to you.

'And Dad…' Carys looked at me, '…will you stay with me to keep me company? They said they'll give you a put-you-up chair in my room.'

'Of course, Cara,' I said, then tried once more – when Ian got back, he wouldn't thank me any for letting his "Cris" go – 'but shouldn't you wait for–'

'Please, Daddy. I don't want to break down. When the ambulance gets here, will you stay and explain to Ian for me?'

She looked around the room at her cherished furniture and paintings, the wedding photos and framed holiday snaps of her and Ian with Abigail, all three happily playing together on the Torquay sands, then she turned for the door.

'I'll only be a minute, Dad. I just want to say goodbye to my home.'

And that's how it was.

She went around all the rooms, closing each door behind her to be alone with her thoughts, spending the longest time in Abigail's room from which she emerged with red eyes. But I didn't hug her, I knew she wouldn't want me to, or she'd have broken down.

And then the ambulance came and took her away.

- thirty -

I don't want to talk about those last months, except to say she was the bravest person I've ever known. That's not to say Rachel wasn't brave, she was. Very. But Carys was only twenty-nine, with a husband and baby she adored, and she should have had many more years to enjoy them.

She didn't once complain. And her daily joy when Ian brought her "little sixpence" in to see her, made the looking after her a strange, heart-rending, sort of privilege.

Not that she didn't cry, she did. But not often. And when she did it was only after Ian and Abigail had left. She'd wait for the door to close, then hold out her arms to me, wanting to be held, and I'd rock her while she sobbed her heart out on my shoulder, wanting so much to live for them.

On two evenings a week, Ian would return early to be alone with her and hold her through the night. And I'd go to spend some time with Abigail and whoever was looking after her, either Anne or Donna.

As for Meryn, well, I'd have been such poor company, I agreed with her suggestion that it would be best if we kept in touch just by phone. Except catching her was mission impossible. That machine of hers was always switched on, so I'd just leave a message. Though goodness knows why, what can you say to a machine, except repeat yourself, then wish you could ring back and wipe it off, except you can't. And instead of talking to her, needing to share my inner-most feelings with her, even though she was miles away, I'd have an early night instead and be back in the hospital first thing the next morning – to let Ian return home for his Mum or Donna to get to their offices by nine, and, of course, to spend the day with Abigail.

In the first month, if the sun was shining, I'd wrap Carys up warm with a rug and take her in a wheelchair for a walk around the gardens. We'd sit under the hanging branches of a large, leafy willow tree and talk – the "do you remember when we…" kind of talk, just like with Rachel, reminiscing about so many happy memories – or we'd just enjoy the balmy air, Carys grasping my hand in silence, silences so rich and enveloping we understood each other so well.

Every moment was precious, even though I was being torn apart from inside.

But as Christmas approached and the weather grew colder, Carys got frailer, too weak to go out, and was confined to her room.

And then to her bed.

That told us the end was near.

She didn't say anything to me so as not to upset me, but she knew.

She knew all right, I could see it in her eyes.

That longing look as she gazed at Ian…and Abigail…and me…with such love, tracing our faces with those deep hazel eyes of hers. Rachel's eyes.

It was like a knife in my heart.

During those last weeks, when she was asleep, I'd go and sit on a bench under the same willow tree. And think cruel thoughts. I didn't want to think them – tried my damnedest to fight them off – but they persisted in invading my mind.

I'd not seen my mother since that party in *Plas-ar-Hendir* to celebrate the result of Carys's first chemo treatment, but she'd recently had a stroke and was now in a nursing home, not even recognising Matthew. And as much as I loved her, staring into space not knowing who or where she was, I'd brood to myself. Yet here was Carys, one third her age, dying before her in full possession of her mental faculties, and a loving husband and adored baby to live for.

And them needing Carys just as much.

It just didn't make any sense. No sense at all.

Then one day someone sent Carys a large bunch of daffodils.

I don't remember who, or where they got them from out of season, but for Carys they were as much a miracle as the daffodils awaiting her Mum's home-coming, seeming to fill the room with their gold, so lifting her spirit that she regarded hers as from God too, and made the same promise her own.

Until then, she hadn't given up hoping for a different miracle. A healing miracle. Her own church was praying for one, and so was she, reminding God of His promise: *"whatsoever you ask in my name it shall be given to you"*, and that *"if you have faith you can move mountains"*, and all she wanted moved was a tumour, a speck in comparison.

But after the daffodils her prayer changed to *"nevertheless not my will be done, but Yours."* And from then on she was completely at peace. The way she saw it (I didn't, only twenty-nine, with so much to live for, I could see no purpose in it, no great eternal plan in it at all) if it was God's will for her to die, then she was ready.

December 25 came and went, Carys clutching my hand as she half slept, wanting so much to be home with Ian, seeing Abigail's excitement as she opened her first real Christmas presents.

Then came New Year's Eve.

Knowing it was their last together, Ian asked to spend it "alone with Cris".

And so I rang Meryn.

That answer machine switched on.

I left her a message on it.

And went to see the New Year in with her.

- thirty-one -

Meryn was all dressed up as usual. Except it wasn't for me.

We stayed standing in her front room as she explained that she'd been expecting "yet another message" from me saying Carys was too ill, and I was going to have to stay with her instead.

And so, not wanting to see the New Year in on her own, she'd half promised to go to a new neighbour's party, which was also a house-warming to celebrate his recent moving in.

Half promised – all dressed up?

And "*his*" moving in? *A man's?*

'He's been so busy settling in he's not had time before, and thought he'd combine the two. He's also invited some other friends.'

'Sounds like you know him well?'

'As it happens,' she said, 'he called here the day he moved in, asking to use my phone; his hadn't been connected. He's recently divorced and looked so tired, being on his own, nor eaten, that I offered to make him a meal. He took me out to dinner next day to say "thank you", and we've gone to the cinema a couple of times since then. As company,' she added, 'nothing more.'

A couple of times! I thought, recalling the answerphone always switched on, over the last two…three…four months.

'*When* did you say he moved in?'

'Three or four months ago. You'd like Rob.'

Rob, not Robert.

'He's been very considerate, inviting me out some evenings, instead of being in the house on my own. But there's nothing more to it than that.'

Maybe…still, I could sense (as well as see) she wanted to go to the party. And so, realising how much her life had been on hold over the last two years because of me, especially the last six months when we'd hardly seen each other, I said, fearing her answer.

'So, what would you like to do, Meryn? About us, not about this evening? I'd prefer you to be honest. If you want to end it, there'll be no hard feelings.'

In fairness, she thought about it a moment, then said:

'I think it would be best if we did, Luke, don't you? We've known each other for some time now, and what with everything…well, we've not got very far, have we?'

Only far enough for me to know there'll never be anyone else for me, ever again, I thought to myself. But I would still have done what I'd done for Carys – even if I'd known all along that this would happen.

She was my one and only daughter.

Precious beyond words.

And would always have come first.

'I know it's been circumstances,' said Meryn, 'not us. My feelings for you haven't changed. But after Carys, I can see you being in shock for a long time.'

She paused for me to say something, but there was nothing I could say.

She was right. I would be in grief for a long time.

For ever.

And so I let her wrap it all up.

'I hope we can stay friends, Luke?'

'Sure, there's no reason for us not to stay friends.'

'Thanks, Luke,' she said, pecking me on the cheek. 'And for being so understanding.'

'That's what friends are for,' I said, and went back to Ian's and Carys's hillside home, wished 'Goodnight' to Anne and Tony, crept into Abigail's room and kissed her warm, sleeping face, so unknowing, so innocent of all that was soon to happen in her little world, whispered, 'I love you, little sixpence, sleep tight...'

And went to my room, took a knockout pill and slept the New Year in.

- thirty-two -

Next day, January 1st, the start of a brand New Year, I was awake early and back in hospital before seven.

I didn't know it then, but it was exactly two weeks to Carys dying. Ten days longer than the doctors expected, and just three weeks and a day from making Abigail's second birthday.

Wanting so much to be there for her, she fought it to the end.

She was asleep when I entered the room, Ian had already left to get back home to Abigail. But as soon as I held her hand, she opened those oh-so-familiar hazel eyes, and looked up at me from her pillows, 'Daddy…!' she managed a smile.

'Dad,' she could only whisper, 'I want you and Ian to stay friends.'

'Of course we will, Carys,' my voice faltered.

'Ian says he's not going to marry again. But I want him to. He's too young, with all his life to live. And I want Abigail to have a Mummy. Wait a few months, Daddy, then tell him, *please.*'

'Mmm-mhu,' I replied.

'One thing; she's got to love Abigail…and be nice to her…and be a good wife to Ian.'

'Mmm-mhu.'

I can't speak Cara, or I'll weep. But you're still organising, still bossing, I see. Oh, Carys, you'll never change.

'And I want you to promise me that when Abigail's old enough, you'll tell her all about me, right from the day I was born. I want her to know her real Mummy.'

'Uh-Uh.'

'And Daddy, stay close to her. Ewen and Jessy must too. She's half me, half us. I want her to feel part of our family, as well as a Gannon. And I want her to stay close to Sara and Nathan, too. Promise me?'

'Mm-mm.'

'*Promise* me, Daddy.'

'I…I promise.'

'And that you'll tell her all about me.'

If I can find the will to keep living, Cara.

I knew the end was near the day she said to Abigail: 'Goodbye, little sixpence, *see you in the morning*,' gave her a long, long hug, and put Abigail's hand in Ian's as if to say, 'She's yours, now. Take especial care of her.'

That same day, after Ian and Abigail left, she didn't cry. We just sat there in silence, Carys now propped up by her pillows, eyes tightly closed, and me in my put-you-up chair holding her hand.

I sat there, looking at her, remembering her as a baby a minute old, so trusting, *cwiched* in my arms, clutching my little finger…and remembering the vow I'd made her, that no harm would ever come to her, not if I could help it, and the way she'd rewarded me with that smile, and then fallen asleep.

Now here she was, falling asleep again, but this time there would be no waking up in my arms.

This was her last day on Earth. I knew it; I could sense it. And I felt so helpless.

So terribly helpless, as if I'd broken my vow and let her down.

That evening, Ian returned early to be with her. When he arrived, I didn't say anything to him, it was for Carys to say. And although she'd told Ian and me that she wanted us both to be with her at her end, each of us holding one of her hands, I could tell, as could Carys, by the tone of Ian's voice, his body language with me, that he wanted to be with her on his own. And even though it broke my heart in two not to stay with her – to leave her for even the tiniest fraction of a second – it was right for me to give in to his wish, I suppose. He was her husband yet they'd had so little time together, and what they'd had was mostly dominated by illness. What's more, they would want to say personal things to each other, and to say their own goodbyes in private.

And so, as I leaned over the bed and hugged her for what we both knew was the last time, she gripped my hand and whispered:

'Goodnight, Daddy. *See you in the morning.*'

'Goodnight, *sweet* heart,' I replied. '*See you in the morning.*'

I left them together and walked out of the room, the room that had been my home for three months now, wanting to look back, but knowing that if I did I would start weeping. And I knew Carys didn't want to see me cry.

Instead, I stumbled out of the building into the gardens, found the bench under the willow tree where we'd spent such precious moments together.

And it was then that I cried.

But still hoping Ian would call me back inside, to spend her last moments with her holding her hand as she wanted me to.

An hour or so later, Ian appeared in the back doorway.

And from a distance, said to me, 'She's gone.'

Only that. Just "she's gone". Nothing more.

Maybe he was too choked-up to say anything else, I don't know.

Whatever, I couldn't reply, merely nodded.

And he went back inside and closed the door.

Later, in her Bible, just as in Rachel's, he found her letters.

One to himself, "To Ian".

One "To Abigail, for when you're older".

One "To Daddy".

And one "To my Family".

I don't know Ian's.

Or Abigail's.

Nor do I want to, they're personal to them.

The one "To Daddy" is also personal.

But I'd like to share the one "To my Family", because it tells so much about my precious daughter, about the person Carys was, that she was able to sit alone in her hospital bed, propped up by her pillows, and write her "goodbyes", knowing they were the last words she would ever write to us.

It must have been while I was in the canteen snatching a hurried meal, since I was with her most of the time and never saw her writing them.

Because of the morphine her writing was a little spidery, and her words, in places, somewhat rambling. But it reads:

> *To my darling Family*
>
> *I want you to know how much I truly love you.*
>
> *Thanks for all the joy, the fun, the sheer enjoyment of you.*
>
> *You are the bestest family I could ever have had.*
>
> *Dad, what a "gag" dad! Truly brilliant! I love you. Be strong & enjoy life around you, and when God calls you Home too, Mummy and I will be there waiting for you.*
>
> *Ewen, thanks for being my brother. I have always enjoyed your friendship, and loved being your little "fister", and all the wonderful times we shared. Enjoy & love your family and look after them. I love you, and Jessy, and Sara & Nathan, God bless you all.*
>
> *My darling daughter, Abigail, my little sixpence, how I love you. You're my heart's desire, the daughter I thought I never would have. You are so precious to me. I gave you birth & life. and you will always be a part of me, no one can take that away from us. It will always be special between us. Be happy and we will meet again one day, in God's love, my darling, of that I am certain.*
>
> *To my husband Ian, my Ian, forever you will be my lover and my best friend. I entrust my daughter to you. And my*

loving memory. You brought joy to my life and I have been so happy with you. Life was wonderful and I thank you.

Just to let you all know I have a sense of wonderful peace in my heart.

God bless you all, always.

Carys

xxx

xx

x

What more is there for me to say
Except that no parent expects a child to go first.
It's a pain like no other.
It never goes away. It's always there.
Wanting her back.

- thirty-three -

And now, all I have left of her are memories.

But they're precious memories, some already mentioned, others too many to number, they would take another book to tell. Especially if I was to add to them the memories told to me by all the many who also loved her: Her best friend, Anna. Her others from her school days. Her work pals who say her laughter lifted their spirits even on a "bad Monday". The nurses who cared for her those last months, who told me she always had a smile and a "thank you" for them all. People who stop me on the street still, to say how much they miss her and her bright "hello".

As for me, they keep flashing through my mind's-eye, remembering…

The tiny one-minute old baby *cwched* in my arms.

The pretty poppet in her white lace christening gown.

The toddler taking her first tottering steps towards me with her arms outstretched.

The curly-headed little four year girl in her new uniform on her first day in school.

Dropping off a distinctly nervous eleven year old outside her new senior school.

A month later transformed into a hockey-stick-wielding terror wanting always to win.

And suddenly, before I knew it, a trendy teenager with a very definite mind of her own.

And again, before I knew it, walking down the aisle on my arm in that wedding dress.

Then, with a look of such wondrous love on her face, *cwtching* her own baby in her arms.

But now, in the twinkling of an eye almost, these memories are all I have left.

And videos and photos of her to show to Abigail one day.

And the many letters and cards I received.

All saying the same.

Of how much Carys was loved.

I'm keeping them all for Abigail in a desk drawer in my own home, which I returned to the same evening Carys died.

Ian said he wanted to be alone with Abigail.

Or alone with his grief?

Or just alone.

Whichever, I packed my things.

Gave Abigail a big, big hug.

And after two years away, drove back to my familiar old home.

To be alone with *my* grief.

- thirty-four -

It's five in the morning, I couldn't sleep.

It's only six days since I started this letter, but three years, seven months since Carys died. Tomorrow is her birthday and I'm sitting in my favourite chair by the window, wondering what flowers to get her.

I still can't take it in that she's no longer here.

Smiling. Laughing.

Her infectious gaiety filling the room.

Often when I wake up in the morning I think I can feel her presence, almost as if I stretched out my hand I could touch her, and I attempt to console myself with some words given to me by a close friend who knew her:

'Measure her life and her love by its depth, Luke, not by its length.'

And I try to – but I'd still like to have had both.

Meanwhile, I withdrew the house off the market and from where I'm sitting, the sky is lit up gold by early dawn peering through the pine trees silhouetted on top of a nearby hill. Already the sun's rays are slanting in, creating rainbow patterns across the room. It's making me think of carnations, Carys's favourite flower, every colour I can find, with petals only just opening, so they'll last longer for her to enjoy.

And if I can find them, some daffodils as well…

Ian and Abigail?

I rarely see them any more.

The last time was about seven months ago, six months or so before Abelin was born, when they and Ileana popped in "for just a moment to say hello" on their way from spending the day with Anne and Tony. Ileana especially wasn't very communicative and seemed particularly anxious to get back home before it went dark.

But Abigail was so funny at their wedding, the way children repeat things they hear. Donna was again one of the bridesmaids, Maria, Ileana's sister, the other, and Abigail was the flower girl, aged three ("and a *quarter*, Gaga,") at the time, looking so pretty and so cute. Gracious, I thought as I watched her coming down the aisle, it feels only yesterday that Sara was Carys's flower girl. Now Abigail is Ileana's.

It felt strange.

As if someone was missing.

But enough…

During the reception Abigail ran across to me and sat on my knee.

'You're going on holiday tomorrow with Daddy and Mummy?' I said to her.

'Yes, but don't wowwy, Gaga,' she said very serious, wanting to reassure me, 'it's alwight, cos I'm mawwied now.'

Bless her, I thought, chuckling to myself, but then she said, 'And we got new furniture.'

What happened to the antique heirlooms that should have been yours one day? I thought. 'Mummy sold them,' she said, when I asked her.

Later I casually said to Ian, 'Abigail's told me you've had a change of furniture.'

'Yes,' he replied, 'Ileana wanted a clean sweep.'

'How much did you get for the settle?' I asked him. Over four centuries of loving polish invested in it. 'And the grandfather clock?'

'I did well,' Ian said. 'Eighty pounds for the settle. Hundred and twenty for the clock.'

'The settle was worth five hundred,' I said. 'The grandfather, double that.'

'Oops,' Ian said.

I didn't even ask about the *ford gron*.

The last time Abigail stayed with me – just the one night – was over a year ago. It wasn't long after the wedding, and I was looking after her for Ian and Ileana to move home – twenty miles or more down the coast. He left the Forestry to go to college and Ileana thought it would better for them to live nearer to it and lessen the distance for him to drive there and back every day.

Abigail was then still only three ("and a *half*, Gaga") so I took her to a playground, and *my,* she was *well* able to look after herself, trying everything in sight, climbing back up the slides to the top, rather than use the ladder – a real tomboy.

Foodwise, she loves cheese-on-toast – *just* like Carys used to – cut into soldiers and dipped in tomato sauce (well she did then, I don't know if she still does). And so we stopped for some at a small café I go to, they're so friendly there, and Abigail introduced herself to Helen, our waitress.

'My name is Abigail, Rachel, Gannon,' she said, 'and *this*…' she emphasised, indicating me someone I already knew '…is my Gaga.'

After our snack we went for a walk in the park, holding hands with her best friend Alex. I forgot to mention Alex; she's invisible; but I still had to hold the car and café doors open for her; and be careful not to trip over her; and buy her invisible cheese on toast (without tomato sauce, Alex doesn't like tomato sauce) when Abigail said:

'I love you, Gaga.' Serious pause. 'We best fwends, aren't we, Gaga? Will you phone me after I gone? 'Cos I going to miss you vewy much.'

I miss her vewy much, too.

I miss her taking my hand and taking me to her bedroom (I used look after her some nights, until Ian remarried) to proudly show me her latest sploshed painting from "nursewy" hanging up on the wall. I miss her climbing on to my lap and wrapping her arms tight around my neck. I miss seeing her face, her smile, her laughter, all her changing expressions. I miss tucking her up in bed at nights and saying: 'See you later, Abigail alligator.' And her giggles when she says back, 'In a while, Gaga cwocodile.' I miss the patter of her feet running down the landing at six the next morning, feeling as if I've hardly had any time to close my eyes (when promising to see me "in a while, Gaga cwocodile", she should have added "short") and her face peeking around my door to check if I'm awake. Seeing I am, she comes in, climbs into my bed and snuggles up to me and asks, all very serious, 'What shall we play, Gaga?'

'I don't know, little sixpence. You choose.'

'I know! Let's play "I Spy". I'll start, shall I, Gaga?'

'Yes please, angel.' *For some reason, I'm not thinking too clearly at the moment.*

Drawing a deep breath, she looks around the room, and finally decides.

'I spy something beginning with Cuh.'

'Curtains?'

'No.' Giggles.

'Carpet?'

'No.' Hand to her mouth as she tries to control her mirth.

'Coat?'

'No.' A touch of increasing excitement in her voice now as victory draws near.

'Oh, you're too good for me, Abigail. I give up.'

'Mirror!' she can hardly wait to blurt. 'I good, aren't I, Gaga?'

'Oh, yes, you're very good, little sixpence. Far too good for me. I'd never have got mirror.'

At which she snuggles with triumphal pleasure even closer to me.

I love this precious little bundle to bits.

'Will you, Gaga? Phone me after I gone?"

'Of course I will, little sweetheart,' I said.

And so I do.

The last time was the other evening when she told me, all excited, that she's moving up to "proper school" in September (the "r"s are now "r"s, not "w"s) and that she and Mummy had just come in from buying her a new uniform – "red jumper with my new school badge stitched on it!'", a white blouse with a red and grey striped tie, grey pleated skirt, and…

'I can put them on myself, Gaga! And fasten my new shoe laces!'

She sounded so proud of herself. I'm sure she looks lovely in it, I'm aching to see her wear it. Maybe one day…maybe soon? Perhaps Ian and Ileana will invite me over to their new home for a meal?

Or just coffee and cake? That would do.

Meryn?

I've seen her only the once since that New Year's Eve. It was a couple of weeks ago, as it happens, a month or so after she cut short another holiday to Tuscany – so a mutual friend chose to tell me, I hadn't asked. At the same time her friendship with Rob also seemingly broke up.

If so, I'm truly sorry, but her reason for coming home was that her brother had died from a sudden heart attack. He was a nice man, Aled, genuine, full of humour, I liked him a lot. I'd sent her flowers and a letter of sympathy. And to her mother, Irwen. And Aled's wife, Sian. So, when I saw her, exquisitely dressed as always, that's what was on my mind.

'Hello, Meryn,' I said, catching her up.

'Oh, hello Luke!' she exclaimed, turning around and seeing me.

'I was sorry to hear about Aled.'

Her eyes filled up. There were only the two of them, Aled and her, and they were close. 'Thank you. It was such a shock. Fortunately he didn't suffer. It was just like Dad. One minute he and Sian were sitting in the garden, the next he'd gone.' She recovered herself. 'And thank you for your letter and the flowers. Mum's as well.'

'As long as they were okay?'

'They were beautiful, lasted weeks, and brightened both our sitting rooms. Did you get our thank-you card? And the card saying sorry about your mother?'

My mother died a few months ago, still not recognising Matthew or me.

'Yes, I got both, thanks. How is your mother?'

'Still low. Cries a lot; can't come to terms with it...but then, you know all about losing a child. She said if I ever saw you, to tell you to pop-in for a cup of tea and a chat...Oh, I'm sorry, Luke,' she touched my arm and it felt as if a flash of electricity had shot right up it. 'I haven't yet asked you how you are?'

I recovered. 'Better, thanks, but still missing Carys. They say time heals, except it doesn't seem to, you just have to learn how to cope with it. How was Tuscany?'

'Tuscany?' she flushed. 'Oh yes, it was beautiful, especially Florence, with all its buildings and statues, and paintings. Quite a culture shock. We – er, Gaenor and I – always wanted to see it. You should go there, Luke, you'd love it.'

'If you'll come with me,' I said, 'as a guide to show me around. Separate rooms of course,' I added, pretending I was being light-hearted, except I wasn't. Just seeing her, and the touch of her hand on my arm, had made me feel all nostalgic, wiping that New Year's Eve right out of my mind. 'As just good friends.'

'Oh, Luke,' she said, 'if only we could turn back the clock.'

I was just about to ask her what she meant by that – was it a negative reply, or a positive response, or just a subjective statement? – but she got in first.

'As much as I'd love to stay and chat,' she said, edging away, 'I'm meeting Gaenor for coffee and don't want to be late.'

In that same moment, Gaenor's *"Meryn!"* came floating on the air, and we saw her bearing down on us, in a rush as usual. But I didn't stay to talk, Meryn seemed on pins to be off. And after saying a quick "hello" to Gaenor, I left them and went for my car.

I've thought of phoning her – Meryn, that is – a few times since then, and maybe invite her out for a meal, telling myself that those last two years we went through would have put a strain on any relationship. Yet, each time I've changed my mind and cut the call in mid dialling.

And that's how it stands, at the moment.

But maybe it's just as well, because I wasn't being truthful when I told her I was "learning to cope" with the loss of Carys.

I'm not.

No matter how I try, the ache won't go away.

When I used to go to church, my favourite hymn was: *O love that wilt not let me go*. But the words that keep repeating in my head are from a love song. There's nothing religious about it, but it expresses the way I feel. It goes:

How much do I love you? I'll tell you no lie.
How deep is the ocean? How high is the sky?
How many times a day do I think of you?
How many roses are sprinkled in dew?
How far would I travel, to be where you are?
How far is the journey, from here to a star?
And if I ever lost you, how much would I cry?
How deep is the ocean? How high is the sky?

When you think about it, it pretty much says the same as *'Oh, love that wilt not let me go'*.

They're both about longing.

As much for Rachel as for Carys.

I just can't get away from it.

I think I'll go out and choose the flowers.

- thirty-five -

Today is Carys's birthday and last night I couldn't sleep.

So I'm at my desk early to end this letter to Abigail, before taking my flowers to Heddwen.

But before picking up my pen, last night in the darkness of my room I again thought I heard the same voice whispering, *"See you in the morning."*

Was it my imagination? Or was I sleeping and perhaps dreaming?

If it wasn't…and I wasn't…then whose voice can it be?

Is it Rachel's?

Or Carys's?

Or Meryn's even?

Or maybe Abigail's?

Except there was no "Gaga cwocodile."

It would be wonderful if it was Abigail's, but there again I don't think it could have been. Because last night Ian rang me out of the blue to tell me that Abigail will be calling me "Gampy" from now on, Ileana doesn't like "Gaga", she thinks it sounds babyish. And, they also think it will best for Abigail if I don't see her for a while.

I'm not sure what they mean by "for a while", being that the last time I saw her was still six months ago, when they all briefly popped in to say "hello", and since then Abelin's been born and is now a month old.

Ian says it's nothing personal, they're only thinking of what's best for her, but it seems that seeing me reminds her of Carys and gets her all confused and upset, and leads to her asking all kinds of questions and Ileana thinks isn't good for her, not now they're a new family and the past is in the past, especially now that Abigail has Abelin for a brother.

If it's because of the way I try to answer Abigail's many questions, then I'm sorry, because I try to do so as gently as I can – I wouldn't upset her for the world, she's far too precious – and so, if not seeing me is really what's best for her, then this is how it must be.

I've examined my heart and my conscience and can't see I've said or done anything wrong. I've also asked all manner of people for advice, especially those in similar situations, and read the experiences of others, wanting to do the right thing.

The last two books I read were *Paula* by Isabel Allende, and Tony Parson's *man and boy*.

Paula is a true story, she was Isabel Allende's only daughter, and very ill, being kept alive by a respirator, with no seeming hope of recovery, yet her mother just couldn't let her go, still holding on to her, refusing permission for the respirator to be switched off, praying for a miracle.

man and boy on the other hand is a novel – about a father struggling to decide what's best for his son. To live with his Dad, or with his Mum who walked out on them and now wants Pat back.

I don't want to précis either story, they'd take too many pages. It's enough to say that after a year of mental and emotional torment, Isabel Allende realises the kindest thing she can do for Paula is to let her go. And let her go is what she does.

Tony Parson's character, Harry, comes to the same conclusion about Pat. He loves his little boy with every nerve of his body, every pull of his heartstrings, but Pat is missing his Mum. And when Harry comes to realise the best thing he can do for Pat is to let him live with his Mum, he takes his "beautiful boy" in his arms, holds him tight and tells him what he's decided.

When Pat demands a reason, Harry explains:

'Because it's the right thing for you,' he says. 'Love means knowing when to let go.'

And that's what my mind tells me I must do for Abigail.

Except my heart says different.

I'll give it some thought as I drive to Heddwen.

- thirty-six -

I hope you like the flowers, Carys. I know today is *your* birthday, but they're for Mummy too, as always, and I'll bring some more for you both when it's her birthday next month.

I stepped back and looked at the arrangement. I failed to get daffodils, but amidst all the colours the yellow carnations are reflecting just as golden in the black marble headstone. Above their reflection, RACHEL and CARYS are carved in a similar gold. I read their ages.

Both so young. So very young.

From out of the ether, I hear Topol's rich voice in my ear, singing: "Would it spoil some great eternal plan…" And in my mind I ask the same question.

Would it have spoilt some great eternal plan to have let them live, God? For Carys, at only twenty-nine, to have lived to be a wife and a mother? Or for Rachel at only forty-five, to have known her three grand-children?

Would the world have suddenly stopped spinning?

Tell me, please, because I'd really like to know.

I know it sounds irrational, but I can't stop feeling it's not right for me to be alive when Carys is buried here. That it's against all natural law for a child – a daughter as precious as mine was – *is* – to me, to die before a parent.

When sometimes I bump into one of her church friends, they try to be kind. They say things like: 'She's in a better place and wouldn't come back.' But they've not been here and seen her name engraved into cold stone, nor the year of her passing which has such an awful finality to it.

Besides, how do they *know* she wouldn't come back? At least, for a time. To have been with Ian a while longer. To have seen Abigail grow up. To see her splash in the sea in summer, and run up the beach all wet for Carys to towel her dry. To hold her hand around the shops at Christmas time, and see her excitement at meeting Santa Claus.

Such words as "she wouldn't come back" are easy to say; they're not so easy to live by. Although they're well intentioned, these people didn't hear our conversations when we were alone in her hospital room, or see my beautiful daughter sobbing, asking could she please catch a number 50 bus to her destination…or a 40 even…instead of the number 29 she was put on.

Sorry, Cara, what was that?

How are Abigail and Ileana getting on together?

They're getting on grand. (So I was told by Anne, Ian's mother, when I saw her in town the other day.)

Give Abigail a big hug and a kiss from you?

Yes, for sure I will.

Yes, Cara, a big, big hug. One of your very specials.

How is Ian?

He's fine (again, to I was told). I'm glad you were "so happy" with him and that "life was wonderful". (In that, at least, I can rest content.)

Yes, of course I'll give him your love.

Ewen and Jessy?

Yes, they're fine too, and send their love. They're calling here later today with Sara and Nathan and bringing their own flowers. If I know Ewen, they'll be carnations. He, too, knows how much you loved them.

Sara and Nathan?

They're growing fast, Cara. Nathan's now seven and into athletics. His hero, from watching old videos, is Carl Lewis, and he wins every race he enters on Sports Day, gouging blocks in the earth with his heels and halfway down the straight before the others have even started.

At nine, Sara's more into fashion wear and school discos, but she still believes in Father Christmas – or says she does – and has already listed her presents for him, not in old fashioned writing as you used to do, but on Jessy's laptop and e-mailed it to "Santa's Grotto", Lapland.

E-mailing Father Christmas…

Yes, and with *umpteen* addresses to write to, one of them: santaclaus@twitter", of all things. If only you knew how rapidly everything's changing, Cara, not just in the world itself, but people too, you wouldn't believe it.

Yes, Cara, we are keeping our promise that they will stay in touch with Abigail.

As it happens, last Saturday Jessy took them to spend the weekend with Abigail. It was Jessy who first phoned Ileana to ask if it would be okay for Abigail to stay a few days with them. But Ileana said she was worried about her being so long away from home, and thought it would be better for

Sara and Nathan to stay with them. Jessy rang again on Friday to make sure it was still on and Abigail spoke to her. 'Is Gaga – sorry, is *Gampy* coming, Aunty Jessy?' she asked. 'I haven't seen him for a *long* time and I miss him.'

I miss you, too, little sixpence.

I miss the games of Hide and Seek we used to play, when she'd ask me to close the closet door for her because she couldn't do it herself from the inside, and then I would have to leave the bedroom and count to twenty before I could come looking for her, and of course never find her because she'd hidden herself so well. I miss the phone calls she used to make when I'd almost jump for joy hearing her voice, using phrases she'd obviously picked up in "proper school':

'Hi, Gaga. It's me, Abigail. I'm just calling to see how you're doing?'

And I'd reply in the same vein.

'Hi to you, too, Abigail. I'm doing okay, thanks. Especially now, talking to you.'

But then they abruptly stopped. I couldn't understand why, until I realised she must have been making them – possibly on an extension out of earshot of whoever was babysitting – when Ian and Ileana were out. If so, I didn't realise they were *secret* calls, and hope that when they appeared on Ian's phone bill, she didn't get into too much trouble.

But I still miss them…

When Jessy dropped Sara and Nathan off on Saturday it was raining, so in the afternoon Ileana stayed home to look after Abelin, while Ian took the other three to see *The Muppets, Treasure Island*. It was Abigail's first visit to the cinema and was seemingly so excited by it all. Later that evening, after they'd gone to bed, Ian went up to check on them and found all three fast asleep in the same bunk bed, the top one naturally – with Abigail snuggled in the middle…

Sorry about that, Cara, my mind must have wandered.

Yes, I promise you, they *are* keeping in touch.

I didn't catch that?

No, nor have I forgotten my promise to tell Abigail all about you. I'm collecting everything together. Old cine films converted to video, countless photos of you growing up – up to you in that wedding dress that almost finished me off, do you remember? And snaps of the three of you together: you, Ian, and Abigail looking just like you, playing happily on the Torquay sands.

So, don't worry, I'm storing it all away, even your old school reports, together with lots of anecdotes and a letter I've just written to Abigail. Rather a long one, I'm afraid, but you know me, once I get started I don't know when to stop. But she's too young for me to give them to her now, I don't want to upset or confuse her. So, I'll wait until she's ready, sixteen perhaps, or maybe eighteen, for her to read them…

Yes, I knew you'd agree that that's the right thing to do.

Meryn?

I hadn't meant to tell you, Cara, but we're no longer together.

No, it was nothing to do with you, you have my word. It was just one of those things.

No, I don't think I'll meet anyone again.

Because I'm happier on my own, Cara.

Yes, truly, believe me…

But if I do, it will have to be special. Eyes across a room, all chemistry and electricity. Tom and Meg on top of the Empire State Building, stars popping in the sky. The whole McCoy. Next time, if there *is* a next time, I want to be sure.

I've also been recently thinking of moving to Italy to live. Somewhere between Sorrento and Positano, with the view from my study window looking over to Capri. I've always fancied it. And I can write just as well – or just as badly – over there, as I can here.

I've also worked it out that whenever Ewen and Jessy and Sara and Nathan fly out to see me, maybe they'll be allowed to bring Abigail with them. If so, then even if it's only once a year, I'll see more of her when I'm living over there, than I do over here.

A decided ten points in Italy's favour.

God?

No, Carys, I haven't yet re-found Him.

Yes, Carys, I am trying, I give you my word,

I really am, I want to believe.

I truly do.

Like you and Mummy did.

It's not for the lack of trying, because if there *is* an *Abba* "Dad" God, and a Heaven, up there somewhere, then one day, when I fall asleep for good, I want to wake up in the morning and see Rachel and my beautiful daughter smiling at me, and asking: 'What kept you? We've missed you.' But until then it's all clouded over by what happened. I still can't find any purpose in their passing, and that's as far as I can see right now. After that, it's all confused.

Do I have your letter? The one to me personally?
Yes, as it happens, I do. I was reading it only yesterday.
Read it again? Okay, if you think it will help.

Heddwen's a beautiful cemetery, peaceful, green lawns with shady trees and garden seats under their spreading branches. Whenever I bring flowers, I always stay awhile here and meditate. I open Carys's letter and begin to read:

> *Dearest, bestest Daddy in the world.*
>
> *I mean these words as I've always meant them.*
>
> *I am alive with Mummy, and we will meet again as surely as I am with Mummy now; and of course I send her your love.*
>
> *Daddy, one strength you have IS to be strong. Stay strong for me, and even though I know I don't need to ask you – because I've prayed for you all and I'm sure all 3 of you will be fine – be friends & family always to Ian & Abigail.*
>
> *I wasn't going to write letters to anybody. But when I realised I was holding on to you all, Ian, Abigail, and you, I realised I had to write separate letters to the three of you, letting you go with my blessing into the new lives ahead of you.*

In my prayers I pray for the future of all three of you, and pray & hope for years of fun and warmth for you all together.

God bless you Daddy. You're my gag Dad, the bestest, and will always be so.

I love you so very, very much.

Carys, xxx

ps. Dad, thank you for all you've done for me throughout my life, especially the last 2 years, and for caring for Abigail. I love you with all my heart. Cara

Despite myself, the words always bring tears. They make me imagine her writing them alone in her hospital bed, knowing they were her last written words to me. And Carys knowing – this is what breaks me – that when I read them, she'd be gone. Her words are so positive, so full of the strength that was uniquely hers, never giving up, despite all she'd gone through, and still displaying that same strength in this her last letter, yet knowing she had only days to live.

But today, her words make me feel ashamed of my self-griping, and put everything into perspective. What I did for her was nothing compared to what *she* went through, and for her to have lived I would have borne it a million times over and lost a billion Meryns.

And yet, her letter still leaves a puzzle.

I re-read her words…

Even though I know I don't need to ask you – because I've prayed for you all, and I'm sure all 3 of you will be fine – be friends & family always to Ian & Abigail.

Oh, Carys, I think to myself, I wanted us to remain friends, too. Instead, what's happened is that on the rare times we've met since Ian re-married, it's as if there's a sort of – I don't quite know how to describe it – as if there's a sort of invisible barrier between us, a great unspoken one, in which we're polite to each other, but nothing more, the old closeness has gone.

It's as if Carys was the only bond keeping us together, and now she's no longer with us it's broken, and not just for a while, but for good.

I don't understand it. I just don't understand any of it.

Today was forecast a grey day, but it's turned out sunny, blue skies with only wisps of white. Maybe I should follow its example and look for the bright side, not the gloom.

'Gampy!' 'Gampy!' 'Gaga!'

Still sitting, I spin my head around.

Ewen and Jessy are walking along the path toward me with their flowers – carnations of every hue. Sara and Nathan are with them…*and Abigail is, too, running as fast as her legs will go, and her face all beaming.* Goodness, she's grown tall.

'Gaga!' she shouts again, forgetting all about calling me "Gampy".

The three of them hit me like thunderbolts. And scramble all over me. Somehow, Abigail is on my knee, her arms around my neck. She pulls back and studies my face with that earnest expression of hers, just like Carys's, as if she can't believe it's me.

'I've missed you, Gaga,' she says.

'And I've missed you too, little sixpence,' I manage to reply, thinking of last night's dream and hearing the words "see you in the morning."

It was me – I must have missed the "*Gaga cwocodile*".

'I love you, Gaga,' she says, nestling her face on my chest.

'And I love you, too, little sweetheart.'

What did I say about thinking of giving you up?

No way, Abigail, no way, I must have been crazy to even consider it.

Sara, not to be outdone, pulls my face around. '*We* love you too, Gampy,' she states, very firm. '*Don't* we, Nathan?'

Nathan's too shy, like most boys of seven, to say such a soppy word. But he nods, with a lop-sided grin, and that says it all.

'And I love you both, too,' I said, putting my arms around them. 'Very, very much.'

Yes, I love all three of you. Love you equally, you little imps.

Italy, did I say? Well, maybe a small holiday villa, just big enough for me to take the three of you with me. And maybe Abelin, too, bless him, when he's a little older? I'd like that. But as for living there, forget it. You ain't getting rid of me that easily.

Ewen and Jessy reach us. Knowing how I'll be feeling today, both give me a bigger hug than usual. 'I thought you'd like to see Abigail,' Jessie whispers, 'especially today, so I drove over to get her. It took a bit of persuading, but…well, she's here.'

Oh, dear, tears in my eyes again.

Thanks, Jessie. To quote Carys, you're the "bestest".

Forgive my earlier gripe about *fileo, paternus* and *eros*.

Love is a lovely word. It's so expressive. It doesn't need addition or alteration.

As for my beautiful daughter, what was it Shakespeare said – roughly speaking?

> *So long as I can breathe and my eyes can see*
> *So long lives my love, and this gives life to thee.*

Thanks, Wil. I couldn't have put it better myself

When I get back home, I'm going to phone Ian and Ileana and invite them over for a meal – specially selected from M&S and heated at 200°, I'm not the best of cooks. And a bottle of red wine, Italian. To chat around the table, and try for things to be normal between the three of us.

I know Carys would like that. And it's time one of us made the first move.

Ewen and Jessy stand by the grave in silence remembering Carys, and Ewen his Mum, too. Then Jessy turns to the three tinkers playing "chase me" in a nearby shrubbery.

'Who's for chicken nuggets and fries from MacDonalds?'

Knowing they'll get MacDonalds surprise gifts with their meals, and Mcflurry ice-creams with chocolate chips as well, we get three instant responses: 'I am'…'I am'…'I am,' and three pairs of eager feet turn and start running for the car-park. We turn to follow after them.

I give one last look back at the headstone, almost hidden by the array of flowers.

Ewen notices and clasps my shoulder. He's the bestest, too, Ewen.

Thanks for the letter, *fy annwyl*, my precious, Carys. I always said you were very special.

I'll try my darnedest to prove your letter right.

Meanwhile, my love to you and Mummy.

See you both in the morning.

And to the end of time.

- epilogue -

To the end of time, did I say?

Eternal time…

Or earthly time…

If it was earthly, then just like my Uncle Billy once said to me.

Nothing could have been truer.

Because a week later, Abigail, like a bolt out of the blue, a letter came from Daddy, written in a hurry, he said, saying you were all flying to Romania for him to start his new work amongst the youth over there, and with no time to for us to even meet, if only briefly, and say goodbye.

And that was now over eleven years ago.

Since then, I've heard nothing from you.

Nor do I have your home address to write to you.

Or even your phone number to call you and chat with you.

And earlier this year you were all of sixteen.

And I have no idea what you look like.

Do you still look like Mummy Carys, I wonder?

I hope you do.

I got Daddy's email address from Grandma Jill and wrote asking him could I send you a special birthday present. He emailed straight back saying "yes", but gave me a PO Box number to send it to, rather than your home address.

I airmailed it, a gold wristwatch, finely made, with a gold bracelet, meant to let you know in my way that I still love you. Love you so very, very much. And enclosed a letter saying that.

But I've heard nothing back.

Not from Daddy if it arrived safely.

Nor from you, whether you like it.

And so I wonder have you had it?

And if you have, do you even know it was from me?

Well, whatever, it doesn't change the way I feel about you.

And so I live quietly here in Trewrthymor, still writing.

And hoping that one day my door bell will ring and it will be you.

Until then, my dearest, dearest Abigail, I hope you somehow get to read this letter.

Letting you know that I love you.

Today.

Tomorrow.

And to the end of time.

All my love, forever,

Gaga xxx

Richard Rees

Richard Rees is originally from Wrexham, North Wales, where he had an accountancy practice, but sold it to try to become a writer. This book tells part of his life's story after that, especially about his young wife and his only daughter, both of whom were such great fun to be with, but died of ovarian cancer. A published novelist, he now lives a quiet life in the seaside town of Llandudno, at the foot of the Snowdonia National Park, doesn't drink or smoke or play around, so sounds a bit of a bore, but is gregarious, keeps fit, drives fast, and doesn't play golf.

For more information on Richard's books, including where to purchase them, or to contact Richard, go to

www.richardhrees.com

23932609R00122

Printed in Great Britain
by Amazon